BOOK OF MIRACLES: FIRST EDITION
MARCH 1999

TESTIMONIES OF GOD'S GREAT SIGNS, WONDERS AND MIRACLES

"And these signs shall follow them that believe; In my name shall they cast out devils; they shall speak with new tongues; They shall take up serpents; and if they drink any deadly thing, it shall not hurt them; they shall lay hands on the sick, and they shall recover." Mark 16:17-18

In 1969, when the mantle passed from Elder Beulah White to her fifth son as Pastor of the Pool of Bethesda, who could have anticipated the miracles, signs and wonders that the Lord would work by his hand? Since Bishop Joseph White began his pastorate thirty years ago, the ministry once housed on Fairwood and Fulton Streets in Columbus, Ohio has now become the headquarters of one of the most dynamic church organizations in the world. Located on five of the earth's seven continents, The Church of the Living God International, Inc. is comprised of blood-washed individuals from all races and cultures. Despite the differences, there are many commonalities. All have needs. All have concerns. This book serves as a testament to the mighty and miracle-working power of God manifested in the ministry of Bishop Joseph White. Bodies have been healed. Babies dead in their mother's wombs have been brought to life. Financial blessings have been loosed.

We pray that you will receive faith in God's power as you rehearse these phenomenal testimonies!

Elder Sharon D. Alston

Director of the International Missions Department

MIRACLE HEALINGS

Minister LaRhonda Turner, Resurrection CLGI, San Antonio TX

In July of 1996, a mere two weeks following the great gathering of the saints in Columbus, Ohio where Bishop White taught us on "The City," I suffered a mild stroke. This stroke left me with left body weakness, I couldn't raise my left arm which was withered, lift my left leg, I could only drag it, and the left corner of my mouth was curved and I had what's termed as "aphasia." The only thing I did have immediate remembrance of, was what I had recently heard of the word of God, taught by Bishop White concerning Hebrews 11 chapter and the City, New Jerusalem.

Upon entering the hospital, they took a CAT scan of my brain and found a mass had developed on the brain. After many more exams they diagnosed the stroke as a result of a "complicated migraine," it had clotted and closed off the blood flow to a part of my brain. It was explained that the brain is like jello, once you take a piece out of the mold, you can't put that mold back together, neither can you replace that portion of the brain that has been damaged. After a few days they sent me home, nothing else they could do. They recommended therapy to hopefully strengthen my muscles and produce the ability to utilize my limbs again. But with the understanding that whatever doesn't return in the next 6 weeks, of my memory or usage in my body probably never would. But because of the effectual fervent prayers of the Bishop White and the Church of the Living God, the Lord has delivered me! It was spoken that I would not have a therapy session, that my memory would be restored better than before, and this testimony of God's greatness would be told all over the world, for he had done this miracle for the Church of the Living God, Resurrection and Me! Well, I want you to know that in the 6 weeks that followed I did attend the initial session for scheduling of therapy and the speech therapist couldn't find a category to place me in, though I had limited remembrance of the words or items, what I could remember was too much for them to categorize and place me, so I had a choice to attend therapy or not, of course I said "NO" and when asked why? With broken, limited speech, God will heal me! The therapist looked at me in pitiful unbelief, but Praise the Lord! I've never been back!

Next, was the therapy for my left body, they attached so many weights and computerized attachments to measure the amount of body weakness to prepare a plan of what I could possibly do to strengthen those muscles, needless to say, every time the computer generated results would come up on the screen, they thought something was wrong with the machine because the muscles in the leg and arm which were damaged, read stronger than a stroke victims should have been and I still have the outward appearance of having had the stroke! Needless to say, they questioned the doctors over and over, read my charts and everyone that read the chart from the initial symptoms 3 days prior to the stroke, to the final results said it was just that a stroke! They were baffled!

Finally after returning to my doctor for my final exams, almost 4 to 5 weeks later, Dr. Russo with great reluctance admitted "IT MUST HAVE BEEN A MIRACLE!" something doctors don't like to say. He had been my physician since the admittance had seen the power of God move. My memory was returning, my speech improving and my body functions returning.

All without therapy, without explanation! After many consultations with the other doctors that day, the "team" of doctors, some who had been with me from the beginning, came to the conclusion that I had a TIA, something that resembled a stroke. Now the mass on my brain was no longer there, the technician who read the scan, and the team of doctors who had told me before were highly experienced, good at what they do, had seen this many times before, misread the scan. Say what they will the records speak for themselves, they have tried to explain away the power that belongeth unto God, I know, we know, that it was the hand of the Lord! Yes, the Lord could have healed me under some other ministry because he is God, but I know it was the effectual fervent prayers of My Bishop - Bishop Joseph White, and his faithfulness unto God, that this miracle was given unto me, in the Church of the Living God International. Where Jesus is Lord!

ISAIAH, MY MIRACLE

Elder Marcel Williams, True Faith CLGI, Japan

While living in Jacksonville, Arkansas, Little Rock A.F.B. I was four months pregnant in November of 1994. During one of these checkups the doctor performed many tests on me at this time because I was a high risk patient. As a result of him taking these test (blood test) he found that the child I was carrying had down syndrome. Down syndrome is a congenital condition characterized by abnormal chromosomes. It is when the 21st chromosome has three instead of two. The child is born with slanted eyes, a broad face, a short fifth finger, etc. They took more tests and it still showed that this was so. The doctors spoke with me and gave me the option of aborting the fetus. Of course I was crushed when I learned of my condition. I was speaking to Elder Vicki Johnson and she encouraged me to call our Presiding Bishop, Bishop Joseph White. She gave me her testimonies of her children to encourage me. I took a deep breath and called Bishop White at his home. I was so nervous when he answered the phone but it was like the woman with the issue of blood I needed the Lord to touch me, I began to tell him my situation. He said let's pray. I put the phone on my shoulder and lifted my hands high to God. He began to pray for me. I remember some of the prayer, he said "God heal this man child and make him perfect just like Jesus was made perfect in Mary's womb." I had not known if I was having a boy or girl yet, but after those words I knew. That's what I hoped for. I experienced the warm sensation of the Holy Spirit move throughout my body and it also filled the room. After that I had great peace in my mind and I knew that the Lord had done something for me. I went back to the doctors and they performed more tests along with an Amniocentesis. All the test results came back negative. The doctors were confused so I told them my Bishop prayed for me and God healed me. Isaiah Jordan Williams was born on April 7, 1995 and was made perfect in the womb just like our Bishop prayed. Thank God for my miracle.

Minister Mary Ruffner, Trinity CLGI, Midwest Jurisdiction

During one of Bishop White's Anniversaries, he prayed for Lydia Aaron's grandson. And I told the Lord I wanted that miracle for my grandson. You see my grandson, Arthur was born with a curved spine and he was going to have to have an operation at the age of five or six because he had stopped growing straight. On that Sunday when Bishop White called the prayer line, I took Arthur up, and Bishop White prayed for him. On Tuesday we were at church and Bishop Alexander noticed Arthur was not walking as he usually did and he told Arthur to run up the isle and back, he had been healed. My daughter took him to the doctor for his check up and they told her it appeared that he had the operation but there was no scar. This is one miracle I will never forget. Arthur was two years old and he is now ten and it is as though this miracle happened yesterday. There is nothing too hard for God.

The Falcon Family, South Korea Fellowship Bible Study CLGI, Pacific Northwest Jurisdiction

Kevin, our third child was sick for the first time with pneumonia at the age of twenty months. We were stationed in Germany at the time under the care and leadership of Bishop Lee. The German doctors released him a few weeks later when it seemed that improvement had been made. After only a few days the wheezing and difficulty breathing began again. Although I was scolded by some, I brought Kevin to every church service and put him in every prayer line for healing. A few months later, he still showed no significant signs of improvement. Bronchitis, bronchiolitis and subsequently another pneumonia in a different region of his lungs set in. After we had tried every marketable cure (antibiotics) both my husband and I were exhausted beyond comprehension. Six months had passed since his release from the hospital. At about this time Bishop White conducted a meeting in Germany. Still desperate for a miracle for our son, we put Kevin in the prayer line for healing once again. After our Bishop's departure, Kevin had to be hospitalized again. Then, to our utter amazement, our miracle began to happen. He started to have an enormous appetite. The doctor's said that it was very unusual for a sick child like him. He would eat not only one plate, but two, full of good food.

We began to have hope for the first time. The nourishment caused his body to strengthen and fight off the disease. We're not sure which prayer line brought about the much needed miracle from God.

Of one thing we can be sure of, it is because of the ministry committed to the hands of Bishop Joseph White, of which we all have the great privilege to be a part of.

God Uses his Faithful Servant, Bishop Joseph White to Heal a Fractured Ankle

Elder Charles E. Robinson, Pastor of Gates of Heaven CLGI, 945 Big Bethel Rd., Hampton VA 23666

Bishop Joseph White, Founder and Presiding Bishop for the Church of the Living God International Inc., came to Hampton VA to run a revival from 26-28 October 1998. During his three day revival, a young man by the name of Neil Armstrong came out on Tuesday night. Brother Neil, a senior Airman in the Air Force, was one of the first ever attendees of the Hampton Bible Study. He had also attended a previous Watch Night Service at the Pool of Bethesda. During this night Bishop ministered to him encouraging him to hold on. After service, Brother Neil told Bishop he would be back for Wednesday night as it being the last night of the revival. Wednesday afternoon, Brother Neil fractured his right ankle playing intramural football at Langley AFB VA. Several military members witnessed this accident. While at Langley AFB Hospital, the doctor viewed Neil's x-rays and showed him the fracture. After being released, Brother Neil keeping his word to Bishop White arrived at Heaven's Gate, CLGI about an hour and a half into service with a cast on his ankle and on crutches.

After the ministry of the Word, Bishop White prayed for and laid hands on Brother Neil and called on several witnesses to lay hands on his ankle. He told him that he knew the Lord could do it, because he (Bishop White) had seen him do it several times before, but he also told him that he would do it because Brother Neil had faith believing because he came out to service that night. Only two days later (Friday, 30 Oct 98), Brother Neil had his first follow up with his doctor to schedule for a hard cast. The doctor, being the first to witness the miracle that God had performed through our Presiding Bishop, informed Brother Neil that the fracture was already healing and he wouldn't need a hard cast. The doctor still believed that it may be 2-6 weeks before he would be able to put any pressure on his ankle. That night while he was talking with roommate, Brother Neil felt the Lord healing his leg and told him that he thought he could walk on it and did. The following morning not only was he walking but it was strong enough for him to play basketball and lift weights.

With love, honor and Praise to God

Elder Christiana M Russell, Pool of Bethesda CLGI, Midwest Jurisdiction

In 1982, when I was 9 years old I caught Malaria when my family lived in Nigeria. Malaria is a disease caused by certain parasites carried by the anopheles mosquito found only in Africa, South America and in countries around the equator. It is a non-curable disease which adapts to the individuals own immune system and can cause death.

My blood and immune system were severely affected by the malaria, and the doctors could only treat the symptoms but could not get the real cause of the problem. The doctor's told my mother that for the rest of my life I would have to deal with all kinds of symptoms related to the Malaria. They also said that certain "traits" from the Malaria in my blood could be passed down to my children and possible increase the likelihood of sickle cell anemia which is a blood disease. The same thing had happened to my grandmother because she had Malaria, and she passed the sickle cell trait on to my mother and several of my siblings. It also caused her to have several miscarriages before she had a successful pregnancy. My mother also had Malaria when she was younger and she passed on the trait to me and to several of my siblings. She, like my grandmother had two miscarriages before she had me. She also had several large growths on her ovaries.

I was affected in the same way with Malaria. However, my immune system was very, very weak and I caught viruses easily and the viruses stayed in my system. Most people caught colds a couple of times during the "cold season", but in the course of one "cold season" I would have strep throat two or three times, bronchitis, the flu and the viral infections due to the bacteria that just took "abode" in my body. As I got older it took me longer and longer to get over these "episodes" and sometimes I would be sick for weeks at a time! The episodes got increasingly worse to where I had severe migraine headaches and my monthly cycle would be turbulent for me. I would bleed severely and lose a lot of blood! It made me very weak and very sick. I had become accustomed to living this way, I began to adapt and just got used to the idea of being sick the rest of my life. I had to go to the doctor every six months for a blood work-up, they did several blood tests because I was anemic. My blood always showed a "deficient specification", which is how they marked my chart.

I recently told Bishop White what had been going on for the past 16 years of my life! He told me that I needed to be delivered and that I needed a miracle! I knew that I really did need a miracle because I was now married and did not want to go through what my mother and grandmother went through during their childbearing years. I never really told anyone but Bishop and my husband Elder Russell.

After that I stood in Bishop's prayer line whenever he asked for those who needed a healing in their body!

The last time I received prayer was on Sunday December 27, 1998. Bishop had those who needed a healing to come by the organ and he took us by the hand and prayed for us! On Monday January 4, 1999, I went to my doctor for my six month visit. The last time I went in May of 1998 in Atlanta, GA. They sent my medical records from Atlanta to Ohio. When my blood was drawn they always send it to the lab immediately for all the test and this time, after several hours, the doctor came in my room and looked at me in amazement! **He said my blood was normal**!!! I no longer had a "deficient blood specification", I was no longer anemic and I am now a normal healthy 25 year old young woman! The doctor was really amazed and I just began to cry! My ultrasound came back perfectly normal – no tissue mass on my ovaries, no blood clots NOTHING!!!

Saints, every 6 months for the past 16 years I have been going for blood work and test and suffering in my body! But, God is a miracle worker! It has been 2 months and we are in the middle of winter in Columbus, OH and I have not even had a "sniffle", my cycle has been regular and I have not even had a headache! **GOD IS A MIRACLE WORKER!!!!!!** I thank God for my Bishop and Pastor Bishop Joseph White whom I love and respect as a man of Faith and Power! Thank you Jesus for my Bishop!

Min. Wanda Talley, Pool of Bethesda CLGI, Midwest Jurisdiction

In June of 1996, I attended our annual Christian Education Picnic. I had been to the doctor several times concerning a stomach condition. The final diagnosis was labeled Irritable Bowel Syndrome. Bishop White was conducting afternoon service with songs of deliverance encouraging words from God's word. He was closing out the service with a prayer line. He asked that those who had need to come believing, and as he laid hands to say. "I believe." I came believing and God healed me and I haven't experienced those symptoms again. I thank God for his mercy and grace and his miracle working power.

Thank God

Elder Linda Clark, Pool of Bethesda CLGI, Midwest Jurisdiction

Some years back I developed a very severe case of Eczema on my hands. I went to a dermatologist who diagnosed it and the prognosis was, that I'd have it for the "rest of my life", and that it could only be partially relieved by the medicated cream. It was so bad that the appearance of my hands brought a negative reaction when people would look at them. But I was encouraged by Bishop White through the word of the Lord, to believe God. And I can't tell you when it happened, but the Holy Ghost brought it to my attention that the blistering and puss that had been seeping, had ceased. I realized then that the Lord had given me a miracle, and it's been 24 years!!

Elder Shirley Bailey, Trinity CLGI, Midwest Jurisdiction

I suffered several years with a chronic back problem, due to the lifting and caring for patients in hospitals. In 1994 I was in so much pain, it was unbearable. I went to see Dr. Saul, x-rays of my spine were taken. The diagnosis, "severe inflammation" so bad that my spine didn't appear on the x-ray. There was nothing Dr. Saul could do but give me inflammatory drugs and instructions of what not to do to cause more pain.

Through Bishop White's ministry, hands were laid upon me and prayer offered to God. I don't know when or how God did it, but he did it and I have not suffered any pain in my back, God gave me a miracle.

Sis Rhonda Butler, Pool of Bethesda CLGI, Midwest Jurisdiction

In 1994 I was in a very serious accident I totaled my car and almost totaled my body.

I fell asleep at the wheel and was pinned in. I had to be removed via the jaws of life, and was life-flighted to the emergency room at Riverside Hospital, where I was placed on life support for 2 days. I was not breathing on my own. Bishop White came into the intensive care room (where my life was hanging in the balances) and laid his anointed hands on me and prayed the prayer of faith and I woke up and recognized him and waved to him. I had been on life support for 2 days and had not regained consciousness until he put his anointed hands on me. I was later (I believe the next day) moved to a regular room and the Lord began to heal my body the more and I was discharged from the hospital.

The accident was in 1984, and I've never suffered any problems whatsoever (in my body) because of the accident.

Diagnosis

- Broken Jaw bone (Jaw broke in 2 places, my mouth was wired shut)
- Laceration to my liver and caused by my ribs (liver and ribs collided together)
- Numerous cuts and bruises
- Severed tendons in my right knee cap

Today, I am healthy, all areas of my body are healed.

Bishop White prayed for me at the 1998 European Jurisdictional Meeting.

Sister Stadmir, East Gulf Coast Jurisdiction

He prayed that the LORD would bless me with a car and a house when I got to Florida. I didn't think that I would be able to afford it, a car and a house at the same time. But the LORD blessed me with a car that is paid for and a 2 bedroom townhouse. I still don't know how the Lord worked it out but He did. This was a miracle for me because I could not see it, no way, no how. It would have never happened if I had not been in the right place, at the right time and I had not believed in the man of God. I pray the LORD will continue to bless Bishop White and keep him in good health.

Missionary Thelma Anderson, Pool of Bethesda, Midwest Jurisdiction

On Friday night, back in 1978, I worked in the nursery. Just before service was over I twisted my ankle. On the next day my ankle and foot were badly swollen. On Sunday, I couldn't put on my shoe. I wanted to go to church regardless, so I wore a cut up tennis shoe on my injured foot and went to morning service.

After Bishop's message, he stepped down the front and asked for anyone with a need to come up. I tried to rush to the front and almost fell. When I got there, Bishop prayed a brief prayer and I started walking back to my seat not noticing that the pain was gone and was walking normal. The pain and swelling were gone and I was healed. This is just one of the many miracles I have received through our Bishops prayers.

Missionary, Exhorter Wilma Tatum, People CLGI, Columbus OH, Midwest Jurisdiction

In the fall of '96, playing with children on the floor, I noticed a lump on my hand. I thought it might have been an insect bite. It did not go away. It did not bother me at all, it was just noticeable and not supped to be there. In June, 1997 it was diagnosed as a cyst and I had it removed. A few weeks after the healing completed, another cyst appeared near the scar.

During the General Assembly 1998, Bishop White told us to come up and whatever we wanted we wanted the Lord to do for us, it would be done in Jesus' name. The cyst began to reduce in size and it is gone. The Lord knows how to operate without leaving a scar. The cyst has not returned.

Min. Kimberly Stephens, European Jurisdiction

Min. Kimberly Stephens was diagnosed with Endometriosis in 1992 and had been prayed for by many Elders up until 1995, when Bishop White prayed for her at the General Assembly. She has been healed ever since.

Min. Joan Leary, European Jurisdiction

Giving honor to God, for his manservant Bishop Joseph White. I would like to testify of the miracle I received as a result of Bishop White's prayer. In 1990 I had surgery underneath both of my arms to remove painful cysts. As a result of the procedures, my sweat glands had to be removed along with the cysts. I thought the surgery would correct the problem, but within one year the growth of the cysts returned underneath my arms. In 1997, the cysts returned underneath both of my arms and were so severe that I had to have surgery again to have them removed. The doctor performed the surgery in the latter part of May, removing the cysts, the infected tissue surrounding the cysts and the scar tissue from the previous surgery, leaving me with over one hundred stitches under each arm. The surgery went well and the doctor decided to release me earlier than expected, giving me permission to travel to the U.S. with about two weeks remaining before I could have the stitches removed. I couldn't use my arms at all. A few days before the General Assembly, two medics took over an hour and a half to remove the stitches, at Fort Bragg, NC. The area seemed a little tender and I was given instructions not to do any lifting or raise my arms, but I was allowed to travel to the General Assembly.

While at the General Assembly the incision began to open a little by little and became larger and larger and I was in a lot of pain. We tried anything we could to close the holes that had developed under my arms. One of the sisters, a nurse, Min. Johnson, helped me out by cleaning and dressing my underarms. I showed my husband, Elder Sister Lee and a few others the wounds. By this time my husband felt that it was time to go to the hospital and let them do something about it. But he wanted to sit through the morning seminar first. That morning Bishop White was teaching on the gift of healing. He was saying "faith comes by hearing and that by the word of God". After his teaching, Bishop asked if anyone wanted to receive the gift of healing, and I proceeded to get into the prayer line because I wanted the gift of healing. After Bishop White prayed for me and I started to walk away, he called me back and started to minister to me. Unknown to him, he began to tell me about this lady who had the same condition that I did and how God had given her a miracle by healing her. For whatever reason I didn't go to the hospital that day. The next morning when I woke up for morning prayer I noticed that I didn't have pain underneath my arms. I went in to the bathroom and the hole was closed and new skin had started growing. I screamed out of excitement and showed my husband, and then went to show Elder Sister Lee, and a few others what God had done. God had given me a miracle and to this day there is no scar tissue and I have not had any more cysts.

Elder Meta Chube, Pool of Bethesda, Midwest Jurisdiction

The surgery was in 1995, and in June of 1996 I was still experiencing discomfort from the surgery. The surgery was successful and the wound had healed. The pulling, pain, and discomfort was thought to have come from adhesions developed during the healing process.

One day during the General Assembly of 1996, the Spirit of the Lord was very high after a great seminar earlier that day by Bishop Joseph White. The Bishop was praying, and said the Lord was touching someone in their lower abdomen. The Lord was touching my body. There was a warm feeling in the lower part of my body. It felt as if something lifted in my abdomen and went into place. The Lord touched my body and took away the pulling discomfort. I thank God for Bishop Joseph White for being obedient to the spirit of the Lord and calling out this condition that was in my body.

Ever since that day I have been healed, and I have not had any pain or discomfort since that day. Thanks be to God through our Lord Jesus Christ for touching me that day.

Min. Sheila Mills, New Full Gospel CLGI, European Jurisdiction

I thank God for the miracle I received in October 1997 during the European Jurisdiction Meeting. I had just returned from Waltar Reed Hospital, after having surgery for cancer found in my body. During that surgery they removed the cancer, but the doctors suspected the cancer penetrated into my lymph nodes. I then had to have a second surgery to remove the lymph nodes. Praise God, the biopsy of the lymph nodes came back negative – no more cancer!

However, I developed a bad infection in my leg from the second surgery. I was placed on antibiotics, and I returned back to Germany. The antibiotics did not work, and my leg was red half way down my thigh. The pain was so great, I walked with a limp.

It was during this time that I attended the European Jurisdictional meeting, where Bishop White was ministering. When I came forward for prayer, he asked did I believe the Lord could heal me, I replied, "Yes Sir", and he laid hands on me and prayed. After service that night I had to sleep on the sofa because the swelling in my leg made sleeping in the bed impossible. I slept on the sofa with many pillows propping my leg up. Around 3:00 am that morning I awoke to go to the rest room, and on my way there, I noticed that I wasn't limping anymore. When I went in the bathroom and turned on the light, I checked myself. The redness that was half way down my thigh was gone. I said to myself… "the Lord has given me a miracle!" I woke my husband and showed him my leg saying, "the Lord had given me a miracle!"

To this day, I give God all the praise, glory, and honor. I thank God for Bishop White because he is a great man of God. My miracle is evidence of how holy Bishop White lives in his body. Bishop White is a man approved by signs, miracles, and wonders. And I am a product of it, Praise be to God.

Elder Eric Russell, Pool of Bethesda, Midwest Jurisdiction

Around 15 years ago, I was in a traumatic car accident. The car accelerated off the freeway into a concrete ditch. The impact of the car hitting the ditch, pushed the engine into the front seat of the car. I was asleep in the front seat on the passenger side, with my shoes off and left foot awkwardly pressing against the foot rest under the glove compartment. The impact of the engine coming into the front, broke both of my ankles. The right ankle was a normal fracture, but the awkward angle of my left foot made too breaks "unusual". The inside bone of the ankle broke completely off which basically meant my ankle bone was lying under my foot. Not only did the engine completely snap the bone, but it turned my foot to be outside at approximately a 45 degree ankle. Without immediate attention the blood flow would be cut off. The surgeon used two screws to reattach my ankle which I still have today. The doctor didn't know how it would turnout because it was such a freak break. All he was sure of was that I would always have trouble with it and I would be able to tell what the weather would be, because my ankle would alert me of any changes, especially rain. Then Bishop White came to visit and prayed for me. Once I halfway learned how to walk with crutches and two broken ankles, I came to church and Bishop prayed for me again. The saints say that the cast became very warm, and the bones began to heal. It has been over ten years and as I write this testimonial, my ankles are still pain free. I still even have to watch the Weather Channel like everyone else, so weather changes don't affect. The Lord definitely gave me a miracle through Bishop White and the saints at the Pool of Bethesda.

Thank you Bishop White and Happy 30th Anniversary!

Min. Rozelle Crowder, Trinity CLG, Midwest Jurisdiction

I was admitted to Community Hospital on January 30, 1999, when there was a mix up in my medication. I wasn't given any insulin for two days, but my sugar stayed down. Thanks be to God, I'm no longer on insulin, after two years of taking 2 injections a day. And my sugar has been down with only the pill.

I know Bishop White is a praying man. So you see God has added many years to my life, given me a nice home and delivered me from taking insulin and in May of 1999, I will be coming off the rest of my medication.

Pastor Maxine Barnett, Peoples CLGI, Midwest Jurisdiction

I have received many miracles since I have been with CLGI, under the leadership of Bishop Joseph White. But some are so great and those are the ones that I would like to share with you.

I was diagnosed with Breast Cancer, Bishop White prayed for me and the Lord healed me. I had two strokes and a heart attack. Through the prayers of Bishop White and the saints, I am still here and just had my 65th birthday.

Thank you Lord for all you have done for me. Friends, whatever you do, stay in this Gospel.

Elder Tim Steward, Peoples CLGI, Midwest Jurisdiction

I had a growth under my eyelid. I received prayer on a Friday night and in two days the swelling was gone. Also my cousin, Robert Lee contracted an illness that affected a vital organ and was in severe pain. He received prayer the day before, he was to go back to the doctors for more tests. The Lord heard the prayers of the saints and Bishop White, all the tests came back negative. The doctors told him that the illness was no longer there. Praise God for his GREAT POWER.

Sister Leslie Green, Pool of Bethesda, Midwest Jurisdiction

I had broken my toe and the doctor said I would need to be on crutches for a while. I came to church, Bishop White laid hands on me on Sunday Morning. Sunday night, I came back to service with the crutches, but this time, I brought them to leave them on the bench, for God had healed me between morning service and evening service. I didn't need the crutches any longer, I could walk and there was no pain. I rejoiced and praised the LORD FOR A SWIFT MIRACLE HEALING.

As a young child I contracted a severe case of lead poisoning. The doctors said I would never develop completely mentally. I would possibly be mentally retarded. Bishop said it shall not be. And to this day, I have never had a problem and I am twenty eight years old now.

I thank God for this ministry, and for a man such as Bishop White, a man of Power and Faith.

Elder Rosa Smith, Pool of Bethesda CLG, Midwest Jurisdiction

On Sunday February 14, 1999, Bishop White called out for a healing for someone who was experiencing numbness in their right leg. That person was me, Elder Rosa Smith.

For weeks, I had experienced severe pain and numbness in my right leg. I have no idea what caused this, it just started paining and cramping. Discomfort in the morning, night, and all day. But God with his great love and magnificent power healed me through the anointed man of God.

Bishop White laid hands on me and prayed, before church was dismissed, I was healed.

Sister Tonya Spriggs, Pool of Bethesda CLG, Midwest Jurisdiction

Three years ago the Lord through Bishop White, gave me peace in my mind and in my soul. I had been through a lot in a short period of time moving to Columbus, Ohio. No one in the church knew anything about me, but one Friday evening in April of 1996, Bishop while playing the organ, said to me "The one that makes you cry let them go…" I thought about what he said to me over and over again. Who could he possibly be talking about? He did not even know me. It took me four months to figure out who the Bishop meant. Since then I have been blessed by the man of God, I have had peace with God ever since.

Min. Geronnie Clark, Pool of Bethesda CLG, Midwest Jurisdiction

I was diagnosed with an incurable blood disease. No known cause, no known cure. This is called TTIP, it affects your kidney, and your heart, and uncontrollable bleeding. I experienced a stroke and loss use of my hand and my speech was slurred.

I was attending a Mission Convention in Tupelo, Mississippi, and all of a sudden my body became very weak, so weak that I had to crawl up to the steps to my room. I was rushed to the hospital that evening. I was told I was dying and bleeding and the platelets (clotting factors) in my system were not functioning. My nails, eyes and different areas on my body began to turn black. The doctor said when he looked at my nails; I had already begun to die. My hemoglobin was down to 2, which was supposed to be at least 8 or 9, and my platelets were 2000 and were supposed to be 9000.

Bishop White came to visit me and spoke these words "YOU'RE NOT GOING TO DIE" and then he laid his hands on me and prayed. I began to throw up some type of poison in my system, I began to feel better. I was transported to a Columbus hospital and there I received chemotherapy to build up my blood.

Bishop White and the saints prayed for me continually, in 1988, I received a complete healing from God and I haven't had a problem with this since. PRAISE THE LORD FOR HIS WONDROUS WORKS AND FOR USING THE MAN OF GOD.

Sister Crystal Clark, Pool of Bethesda CLG, Midwest Jurisdiction

At two years old, I developed a blood tumor on my thigh. I had it removed and it came back, when I came to the church, I would get in every prayer line. I had it removed a second time, it returned.

Sunday morning, Bishop White prayed, rebuked the devil and it has not returned since, it has been 8 years and I have no problem with it reoccurring.

Minister Rocita & Brother Bobby Belsher, Trinity CLG, Midwest Jurisdiction

I have two miracles, the first one was in January 1992 during Bishop Carl Alexander's pastoral anniversary. At the end of the service Bishop White did the altar call and then he called my daughter Rochrata (Ta) out for prayer. Pastor leaned over and told him that she was not saved, but Bishop White replied the Lord had me to call her out for a reason. She was about six month pregnant with my oldest grandson Cortez. Bishop prayed that she would have an easy birth, that she would have a healthy baby, and that she would deliver the baby without a lot of pain. Now remember my daughter was in sin at this time. Little did I know, she was having problems carrying. Well her water broke about two weeks later which I did not realize at first. I took her to the doctor and they told me that her membrane had rupture. They immediately admitted her to the hospital. They told us that if they couldn't keep her from delivering the baby, he wouldn't make it, but then I remembered what Bishop said. The doctor told us that if she delivered now that Cortez' lungs will not be developed enough to breathe on his own and that he would be really underweight. They placed Ta in the bed flat on her back with her feet in the air and her head down to try and keep water for Cortez to survive long enough for his lungs to develop. This went on for two weeks and the Lord blessed, because they did an ultrasound on her every day and everyday there would be enough fluid for Cortez to go another day. What is amazing is that she would always lose the fluid at night and in the morning it would build back up. The doctors even said that they had never seen anything like this before, this went on for two weeks. Now at the time they were ready to induce her labor they had set everything up from the incubator to the life support machine and even had a specialist standing by at birth. On February 4, 1992, Ta gave birth to a 6 lb. 8 oz. baby whose lungs were fully developed and no complications. To this day I call him my miracle baby. He is 7 years old, with no health problems as a result of being born 11 weeks early.

The second miracle happened in May, 1997. I was working for the State when I fell on my left knee, not knowing how badly it was injured. I walked on it for three weeks before I went to the doctor. At the time I went my knee was swollen twice its size and I could no longer bend it. They took X-rays and discovered that I had a hair line fracture. They put a knee mobilizer on to prevent me from bending or doing any more damage to my knee. Then they sent me to an appointment to see an orthopedic specialist. I went to see the specialist. The specialist talked about doing knee surgery and I knew deep down that I didn't want to. During the Jurisdictional Brotherhood Meeting on Saturday night they called the altar call. Bishop prayed for me and the next day I took off the knee mobilizer and walked. I went back to the doctor the following week, they did x-rays again and they could not find where the fracture was located. I was only in the knee mobilizer for two weeks. No surgery, no pain and from that point on I have not had any problems with that knee. I just want to say that I thank God for Bishop Joseph White for touching my daughter's life and mine. My family and I pray that God will continue use you, and enlarge the borders of your tent.

Elder Gary A. Watson, Sr. International Director of Christian Education, Pool of Bethesda CLGI, Midwest Jurisdiction

To Bishop Joseph White: (A "True" Man of God)

Giving honor to a "true" man of God, Bishop Joseph White.

Since the day you (Bishop White) introduced Jesus Christ to me, my spiritual path has been enhanced with bountiful blessings. Some of them have not been realized yet, but I know they are with me. I am still learning how to follow "this man Jesus", but you are the perfect example for all to see how a person should follow a good leader.

Out of the hundreds of blessings and healings that have come my way, I want to focus on one that has changed my life. I am not sure as to the date or the year that my problem started, but I do know I had a great problem concerning my kidneys and my gall bladder. For over ten years (as I remember) I had a very discomforting feeling and severe pains in my lower stomach and right side. I had on occasion mentioned it during services when prayer lines were called, and would wait for God's healing to take place. I do know that the Lord heals, as I mentioned years that I have had several healings, and I do know that if He (The Lord) has done it once, he can do it again. My faith is not weak, I do very much so believe in prayer changing things. I have always believed in Isaiah's statement (Isaiah 53:), that the Lord bore many stripes on his back for our healing. I was greatly aware that surgery was an option. At best, this problem was continuing to worsen. I had almost decided to tolerate the pains, and live with it.

I had for years favored my right side, in protecting it during functions, taking care that it would not get bumped, as the pain was present, but calm. I would almost always have an upset stomach. I imagine that my countenance gave away my discomfort.

My family, saints at church, and my pastor, Bishop White would ask me how I was feeling, as they knew I had something going on in my body, but not exactly sure what it was. Bishop White would give me one of those godly bear hugs with his greetings, and noticed in the Spirit that all was not well. He would follow with a "how are you feeling Elder Watson".

My precious wife would continually admonish me to see a doctor, which I did on occasion, but would not always give her the diagnosed alternative "surgery". So about three and a half years ago I had given in to my wife's urging and had a series of tests ordered. Within a fourteen month time span I had gone through EKGs, cat scans, upper and lower GI's, two ultra sound tests, outpatient surgery (to get stomach and kidney tissue samples), and a variety of x-rays, with all giving me no great news.

I am and have always been active at just about all of our church functions, district meetings (at that time), and travels. When a meeting would start, the Watson Family was there. I am so thankful for a pastor who has concern for God's flock, not being a hireling, but a true shepherd. A man that is fully committed to Christ and this divine anointed ministry. A yielding vessel to God, with all nine gifts of the Spirit, that during two different regional meetings, and on various dates throughout the months, has allowed the Holy Spirit to put me on his mind by calling me out for prayer. I am sure that Bishop White has also prayed for me in his private devotions to our Savior Jesus Christ. Once again, I am so thankful for my pastor, Bishop White.

After having three consultations with two surgeons in September, 1997, and looking at the results of the x-rays, and lab reports, I had considered surgery, but I would wait for April 1998, when I completed the great fasting time and the Bishop's Anniversary. The last surgeon told me to have one more test performed, just to be sure he know what he was getting into. In October of 1997, I was told that my diaphragm had a hole in it the size of a large grapefruit, and that the upper part of my stomach was pushed through the opening. He mentioned that if I put off surgery much longer, that part of my stomach shoved through this hole would die and I would very possibly end up with great digestive problems, followed with other lifelong conditions.

In December 1997, the pain and discomfort increased. I realized something had to be done. Wednesday, December 18, 1997 I had gone to a third surgeon who tested me again, in hopes of prepping me for surgery. On Monday, December 29, 1997 (with the great watch services just two days away) my main surgeon wanted to see me to discuss my hospital arrangements that he had set up with my admittance to be the first week of the New Year. But prior to that, I was to get another upper GI on Wednesday, December 31, 1997 at 7:30 am.

On the following night (prior to watch services), Tuesday night, December 30, 1997 Bishop White called me out for a special prayer, no one else, just Elder Gary Watson Senior. (I must add that I had not mentioned my last meetings with the doctors to the Bishop, he was led by the Spirit to pronounce a blessing on me). Bishop White asked me to come forward and stand with my hands uplifted towards Heaven. He asked me if I believed that our God could heal and deliver. If I believed with unwavering faith, then it would be done unto me. I received just what Bishop White had on that night preached about "having faith in the One who has all power". I felt a change in my body, a feeling of wholeness in my body, something I had not felt in years. After a dynamic prayer, which lasted about 5 minutes, I was told to return to my seat, and once again believe on the one who has all the power. That night was a miracle night for me, as it appeared that all of the discomfort, pain, and nausea associated with condition left me. I had been transformed from location A (sickly) to location Z (healed).

I could not wait to go to that 7:30 am testing the next morning for the upper GI. I spent two hours under machinery, drinking barium sulfate, and having x-rays of my insides while I looked at the television monitor following the fluids traveling through me. After several x-rays, the technician asked me to wait in the examination room while he would get the doctor to review my films. After a long, cold ten minute wait, the doctor came in and asked me why I was sent to the lab, and what my ailment was. I said you have my x-ray requests from the surgeons office, what do they say? Following a question and answer period, I mentioned what the reason for me being there was. The doctor was puzzled, and had me to go into another room with a rotating table (it would position me flat on my back and then gradually lift me forward until I was on my stomach. All through this rotation I was to drink a formula, and hold it in my throat and esophagus. I made it, and headed back to the cold room. The doctor with the technician appeared once again, stopped and looked at me, looked at the photos, and finally said I don't see any trace of abnormality in these x-rays. I asked would you repeat that, and showed me the shots. All three of us looked at the shots, and I had just to say I have been healed, I just got a miracle from God through Bishop Joseph White. The doctor would not go any further as to what he sees or doesn't see, but referred me back to my surgeon.

Now I couldn't wait for the evening services to come. New Year's Eve watch services. I had received a miracle and had no doubts about it. Needless to say I had a testimony.

Following the scriptures, I had to show myself to the priests (in this case the physicians). So a few short days later Wednesday, January 7, 1998 at 3:00 pm. As I sat in the surgeon's office, I was anticipating his opening the door and me bursting out with I've got my miracle, and no surgery this time doc." (The doctor knew that I believe in God's healing power). He opened the door, and before I could start my witness, he said "No signs of the hole, no sign of the stomach sticking though the diaphragm, no surgery." After that we had our talk, and he said get rid of the hospital admittance schedules, and he would cancel all plans for the surgery.

I love Bishop White as he is truly a man of God, and can get a prayer through directly to the throne room of God.

I am so ever thankful that the Lord placed me in this great ministry, under the blessed guidance of a humble servant, Bishop White, a "true man of God."

I very graciously confess that there is no other ministry like this ministry under the Godsend Bishop Joseph White as Founder and Presiding Bishop of the Churches of the Living God International, Incorporated.

I am greatly indebted to you and our Lord and Savior Jesus Christ.

My prayers go up daily for you.

Minister Linda Tapscott, Pool of Bethesda CLG, Midwest Jurisdiction

When I came to the Pool of Bethesda little did I know that erratic cells were growing in my body. The first miracle that I received under this ministry was salvation for my soul. Deliverance from the powers of darkness and the bondage of sin.

For one year my physical condition was misdiagnosed. Three minor surgeries and several doctors later, I was found to have nine tumors in my body, one on a major artery!

Bishop White prayed for me. He reassured me that everything was going to be alright.

When I went into the hospital I was no longer fearful but confident in God, praising God for Bishop White's great faith and prayers.

The surgery was successful and the doctor said in his own words "THAT IT WAS A MIRACLE."

Aaron Alston, 7 years old (Elder Sharon Alston's grandson), Pool of Bethesda, Midwest Jurisdiction

In 1998 Aaron began to carry a high fever, his joint were sore, his skin was peeling and his heart was beating irregular. The doctor diagnosed Aaron with scarlet fever, and he was suffering from the side effect of this illness. We were told Aaron was in serious trouble, his immune system was very weak and he would catch everything that he came in contact with. The doctors put him on medication and said he had to take it for a year. I kept putting Aaron in the prayer line, he really wasn't getting any better. I told Bishop White about Aaron and he told me to bring him to the next service, it was a Tuesday service. At the end of service Bishop told me to bring Aaron up and he laid hands on him. (Aaron had already told his mother before he went to church, that he was going to get healed). After church, he told her "Mom I got healed at church tonight", and then he passed this same information on to all the rest of the family.

It has been one year since this has occurred, and Aaron was taken off medication soon after the prayer, his joints have not hurt, and his immune system is strong now. We thank God and Bishop White for blessing us.

Elder Carolyn Taylor, Pool of Bethesda CLG,

Southwest/Midwest Jurisdiction

I was diagnosed with sarcoidisis, a lung disorder, in the winter of 1989, after not responding to penicillin for what the doctor thought was bronchitis.

For two years I suffered with this and was on prednisone which gave temporary relief. In the General Assembly of 1992, Bishop was praying for us after his Wednesday seminar. The Lord miraculously healed me and this had been confirmed by the doctors for the last six years.

Bishop T. L. Lucky, Sword of the Spirit CLG,

Northeast Jurisdiction

In July 1993, Bishop White and several members of the Pool of Bethesda came to the first official service of Sword of the Spirit. Members of my family also traveled from New Haven, Connecticut to attend. Torrential rains and horrendous traffic turned their three-and-a-half hour trip into an eight hour ordeal. When my mother finally walked into the service, Bishop White had already begun to preach. As she found her seat, Bishop interrupted his message and began to say that someone had a problem in their right breast. He suggested that the person come when the prayer line was called because he didn't want to embarrass anyone. He then continued with this sermon. Unbeknownst to anyone in the room except my immediate family, my mother had recently been diagnosed with breast cancer. But no one other than my mother knew in which breast the cancer was located. Bishop White prayed for her, as she was due to undergo surgery within a few weeks. The extensive and complex surgery often requires chemotherapy and radiation treatments. To this day, my mother is completely healed and healthy and has not undergone any further surgeries or radiation therapies.

Elder Crystal J. Lucky, Sword of the Spirit CLG, Northeast Jurisdiction

At the 1997 New Year's Eve Service at the Pool of Bethesda, I went to Bishop White for prayer because I had been diagnosed with a tumor located under my right nostril, which had been growing in size. I underwent surgery the first week of January 1998 to have it removed. The doctor's report was that he removed a cyst instead of a tumor as the MRI test had indicated. Truly, the Lord worked a miracle for me!

Miracles from Bethesda CLG, Midwest Jurisdiction

- Sister Michelle Battee had a curved spine. She had to undergo major surgery and the Lord had to guide the doctor's hands. The doctors said it was going to take weeks for her to walk and she would have to take physical therapy, but less than a week after surgery, the prayers went up and she was walking in about 3 to 4 days. The Lord blessed and her stay was short.

- Sister Alexis sprain her foot. One day she was walking in school with stack shoes and she twisted her ankle and we came to church at the Pool and Bishop White was watching her and in the Spirit knew something was wrong and called her up for prayer and the Lord healed her ankle.

- Bro. Kjuan just recently came to church and started having chest pain and was crying because of the pain. During Christian Education Pastor Battee took the time to pray for him and in a few moments he was healed by the blood of Jesus.

- First Lady Michelle Battee was blessed in the Missionary Convention. She went to the doctor and found that her fingers were broken. Bishop prayed for her hand and she felt the warmth as he pray and she was healed that very day. She was not able to button or zip or hold anything with that hand and after the miracle she was able to do all these things again.

- Rev. Serina Brooks receive her blessing when the Lord healed her finger. She smashed it in the car door and fractured it in 4 different places. She went to the doctor on Monday and another x-ray was taken, and the finger did not have fracture at all. Nothing but God's Power.

Min. Ava Jackson, New Life CLGI, Lakenheath England

On 27 May 98, I was diagnosed as (1) having a moderate sized left ovarian cyst and (2) ruptured follicular cyst right ovary. The cyst on my left ovary measured 4.49 x 3.53 x 4.67 cm and increased the overall size of my left ovary to 5.61 x 3.98 x 4.7 cm. My right ovary demonstrated a cystic component measuring 1.09 cm. Some paraovarian fluid was noted on the right side suggesting recent rapture. The right ovary measured 2.1 x 2.3 x 1.86 cm.

On 6 Aug 98, during the European Jurisdiction Meeting Bishop White began to minister to the people. I was sitting to Bishop White's right on the third row. The first two rows were completely filled. As he began to minister to the people, he said Sis Jackson, I can't see your face but I do see your stomach. He told me to step out into the aisle and lift up my hands right where I was. I knew that I had the cysts but Bishop White didn't know. I believe that's when the Lord gave me my healing miracle.

On 23 Oct 98 when I went for a follow-up the cysts were gone.

Min. Howard Hammond, Resurrection CLG, Southwest Jurisdiction

Last November, I had a surgical procedure called lithotripsy performed on my right kidney. The procedure used sonic pulses to break up large kidney stones into fragments so that they can be expelled from the body through the urinary tract. I was given general anesthesia and placed on life support systems for the 2 hour procedure. At the end of the procedure, the medical staff found it extremely difficult to wake me after the recommended recovery period. All of their manual stimulation techniques proved ineffective and at the end of a four hour period, I was still unconscious. The entire physician team was baffled. They did not know what the problem was. At the end of their list of things to try, they administered a mixture of glucose (blood sugar) and water, and it worked. I regained full consciousness in under two minutes with no recollection of what happened. Because sugar was successful in reviving me, diabetes was a strong suspicion. I was hospitalized for two days in the intensive care unit and for two additional days on a observation ward.

I phoned Bishop White when I got home to tell him about my experience. My doctors had planned a series of tests to identify what the source was. I expressed my concern over the whole matter. After asking some specific medical history questions he said, "I really wouldn't worry about it. I don't believe that it is diabetes. You know sometimes they can give you too much anesthesia and it takes you a little longer to come around again… Our (the saints) bodies are clean and not used to drugs so our tolerance for those things are generally lower." He then went on to share how one of his sisters was given too much anesthesia years ago and she had a difficult time waking up as well. He assured me that my situation was the same but encouraged me to allow the doctors to take their test so that God can prove Himself. I asked him to keep me in his prayers and that he said he would.

In December, I went to visit my doctor for a follow-up appointment. He felt that I had suffered from neuroglycopenia, which is a sever manifestation of hypoglycemia (low blood sugar). Neuroglycopenia changes can begin at mental disorientation but if left untreated can progress to a coma, and even death. The lab tests and their various values from November did not confirm diabetes but instead suggested the presence of insulinomas. Insulinomas are small tumors on your pancreas that increase the normal levels of insulin in your blood. They can be malignant (cancer) and the only way to be sure is to have major abdominal surgery, remove them, and test them. The medical staff was sure that this was the problem and signed me up for a battery of tests for the month of January.

I went back into the intensive care unit in January 1999 for a recreation of November's events. I was not allowed to eat anything for three days and nights and my blood was drawn every hour. The doctors gave me mental evaluations every two hours hoping to see changes in their search for a concrete diagnosis. There were no changes and every lab test was within normal ranges. I never lost consciousness or had any mental status changes. It didn't make medical sense to them. But it made good sense to me. The Lord had healed me completely.

Nevertheless, they still believed that I had the insulinomas and consulted with me for the strong possibility of exploratory surgery in February. There was one final test using and x-ray device and contrasting dye. If they were present at all, they would surely see them.

In February 1999, the test was performed. It was negative. The scan of my entire pancreas was clear and free of any indication of tumors. I have not had the need to take any of the medication prescribed since January. Praise the Lord! After 50 blood tests, 40 neurological evaluations, 15 consultations with 8 different specialists, and 7 x-rays it was over. The Lord ruled out their suspicions of diabetes, insulinomas, and abdominal cancer. During my final talk with my doctor he said, "Howard, I think that what happened in November was a combination of the strength of the drugs used to put you under and the moderate case of hypoglycemia you have. It was probably too much for you." I was floored by his use of some words that Bishop White had encouraged me with months earlier. I thanked the Lord for His power and praise him for it every day.

Note: Throughout this 4 month period, the Lord also ministered to me through Bishop Mester, Bishop Smith, Elder Sis. Mester, and the Pastors of Resurrection. I choose to believe that the effectual fervent prayers of Bishop White and all the saints resulted in a miracle in my life.

"THE RESULTS OF BISHOP JOSEPH WHITE'S PRAYERS FOR ME"

Date: June 1986

Place: Pool of Bethesda, CLGI

Illness: Broken Ankle

It was a beautiful summer afternoon in Columbus, Ohio. All the saints were outside in the church parking lot after noon-day prayer. I remember it all so clearly. The day was Monday. The church parking lot had not been paved; there was only gravel. At the age of fifteen, I was full of energy. So there I was, running around playing 'tag' with William Clark Jr. and Tommy Moore. While chasing after Tommy Moore, I tried to make a sharp turn around our big brown van. Before

I knew it, I had slid on the gravel and my foot bent so that my ankle bone completely touched the ground.

I yelled with a loud voice, and my parents came over to see what happened. At that time in my life, I had a terrible habit of faking accidents and sickness. So my parents told me to get up and sit in the van until they were ready to leave. After we left the church, we went to my grandmother's house. When I tried to get out of the van, I found myself having to hop on one foot. My parents said to me, "Stop acting silly and walk like you've got some sense". However, I couldn't apply any pressure to my left foot. After we entered my grandmother's house, my grandmother asked me, "What's wrong with your foot?" My mother replied, "Moma, ain't nothing wrong with Gary's foot, he just being silly!"

On Tuesday afternoon, my parents finally took me to the emergency room at either Riverside Hospital or Grant Medical. After having x-rays taken of my left foot, the x-rays showed a portion of the bone on the outside of my left foot (about half the length of a credit card, and the width of a stick of chewing gum) had broken off from rest of the bone. The doctor proceeded to put cast on my left foot. The cast extended all the way up to my knee. He told me and my parents that I would have to leave the cast on my foot for at least eight weeks! All I could do that moment was think of all the fun that I'd be missing for eight long weeks. That meant no swimming, playing basketball (at the Boys club), and no playing football; which I just had to do! Well, my parents took me home so that I could rest my foot. I was told not to put any pressure on it. Before I knew it, it was time to go to church. I remember thinking, "What are the other young people going to think, when they see me wearing this cast?" I had never experienced having a broken bone before, so I felt sort of weird. When we arrived, the service had already begun. The last thing that I wanted to happen was for us to be late for service. This meant that everyone would be looking at me as I walked into the sanctuary on my crutches. My father helped me get situated as I sat down on the last row at the back of the sanctuary. After the devotion, youth choir, and the preaching had ended, the Bishop began to minister to those who were sick. That night, (as many other services), the Bishop reminded me so of Jesus Christ. He ministered exactly the way Jesus did while he was here on earth. I can't remember who the Bishop prayed for before he prayed for me, but I do remember when he called my name. He said, "Brother Gary, what's the matter with you? Why do you have those crutches?" At that time, my father helped me up to the front of the sanctuary where the Bishop stood. I remember the host of ministers (some who are now elders) gathered around me. The Bishop was standing in the midst of them. I began to tell him what happened to me, and all of a sudden he interrupted my story by saying, "Oh it doesn't matter what or how it happened, the Lord is able to fix it!" So the Bishop and all of the ministers proceeded to pray for my left foot. Keep in mind, I was not saved at this present time, so the Lord must have had mercy on me that night.

As the Bishop began to touch my foot, something very very strange started taking place. My foot had begun to get warm – very warm. I can remember myself trembling at what was happening. Then the Bishop said, "The cast is getting warm!" He then asked me if my foot was getting warm; I told him, "Yes sir". At that time, the Bishop told the saints to begin to worship and praise the Lord for what he (the Lord) was doing for me. After the Bishop and the ministers prayed for me, the Bishop told me to try to walk on my left foot without the crutches. As I obeyed, I noticed that the pain was "COMPLETELY GONE"!!!!! The saints began to rejoice and praise the Lord for giving me a miracle!

The next day (Wednesday) I walked around the house all day. My mother said, "Since your foot is healed, you can get back to cleaning the house!" But it didn't matter, I knew for a fact that I was healed. My next scheduled examination was on Thursday afternoon. So on Thursday afternoon, my parents took me to the doctor's office. Our family doctor wanted to know why we were back so soon. My mother told it all. She told him all about the Bishop and the ministers praying for my foot to be healed. He looked as though my mom was crazy and set up an immediate x-ray. When the x-rays were developed, the doctor couldn't believe his eyes! He called a couple other doctors into the room. He immediately showed my parents the x-rays of my left foot. God, through His perfect son Jesus Christ, had placed a "BRAND NEW" bone in the same exact place, where the other bone had broken off. Not only that, but there was no line-of-separation showing where the old bone had been replaced by the "NEW BONE!" My mother yelled, "Thank you Jesus!" She then said to me, "Gary, the Lord gave you a miracle!" I was so over-whelmed with joy that I started trembling again (just like when the Bishop and the minsters had prayed for me).

Lastly, a female doctor took hold of my foot, and began to push, pull and twist my foot and ankle to see if I would feel any pain. I could tell by the expression on her face, that Satan was upset at the miracle which God through his son Jesus Christ had performed. Oh, I forgot one important part. Before the doctor took x-rays of my foot, they agreed to cut the cast off. Besides, they had no choice. After all, I had been walking around on my left foot so much, that the bottom of my cast had begun to crumble and break apart. They also took an x-ray of my right foot, to compare it with the formerly injured left foot. When we arrived at church on Friday night, my mother testified of the miracle that I had received. After she finished testifying, the saints went up in a high praise!

Thank you very much Bishop Joseph White for praying for me; thus enabling me to receive my "FIRST MIRACLE AT THE POOL OF BETHESDA!" I LOVE YOU VERY MUCH BISHOP!!!!

Still in God's service – Thanking him daily,

Min. Gary L. Watson Jr., CLGI Min. of Music (February 9, 1999)

Rev. Mary Bracy

Praise God for the Gospel that saves and for God's servant who has been spreading the Gospel for thirty (30) years. Not only did the Gospel save my soul from the power of sin and death, but also delivered me from me addiction to cigarettes for over twenty (20) years and from Valium for five (5) years.

The Power of God was so strong with Bishop White that when he spoke God's word it was confirmed with miracles. I went to the Bishop with a serious problem that I was having in my stomach and other complications associated with my stomach. Bishop White told me not to worry. He said it would be no serious problem but to go to the doctor and get a checkup. PRAISE GOD! The result was no serious problem. I also remember having a large mole on my face. After Bishop White spoke God's Word he laid his hands on it. A few days passed and the Holy Spirit spoke and said, "Look at your face." The mole had disappeared.

Bishop White may you have many more years serving God, and spreading the Gospel.

Rebecca Hammond's Miraculous Miracle

In the summer of 1985, Rhonda, Eric, Michael and I began our travel home to Columbus, Ohio after a full active day at the Cedar Point Amusement Park.

About an hour and a half into the ride, Rhonda fell asleep. The car veered off the highway into the field and slammed into the culvert. The accident was described as devastating, by a witness account. *The emergency vehicle rushed me to the nearest hospital. My case was so severe and life-threatening that I was later transported to a hospital in the Columbus area.*

The doctors described me as being in a state of shock, with internal bleeding and swelling of the brain. In addition, I had a right knee and left ankle sprain, with a partially collapsed lung. Furthermore, I was in a coma for four days.

Bishop Joseph White, the great man of God, with much faith and power prayed for me continuously. It was because of his prayers that I survived this accident.

THIS WAS TRULY A MIRACLE!!!

Thank you Uncle Joseph! Your prayers brought me out of the coma and changed my condition.

With much love your niece,

Minister Rebecca Hammond

IT TOOK A MIRACLE

Submitted by: Elder Harriet Watson

There are so many miracles that have taken place since **The Watson Family** has been at the Pool of Bethesda. It is difficult to choose from the numerous blessings and miracles that God has given us through his precious and glorious ministry under our **GREAT Apostle, Pastor and Bishop, Bishop Joseph White**. I will try and choose some from among many miracles. Of course, the greatest miracle is the

Miracle of Salvation that God has given to our family. We will never forget this as long as we live. The Gospel of Jesus Christ that set us free from the Law of Sin and Death.

Miracle of Conception: Eld. Watson had gotten married, we desired to have another child. I had been having some gynecological problems but I did not think that they would have kept me from getting pregnant, but they did. The doctors said I had numerous problems. One day Bishop White was giving a sister words of encouragement regarding getting pregnant. I was sitting there listening to Bishop (at this time he was Bro. Joseph) when I thought to myself that I would take these words of faith for my own situation. Time passed, but I was still unable to conceive. Being young in the Lord, my faith began to waiver. Finally I went to the doctor and he began to try to calculate the best time for me to conceive. We went through this procedure for a while. I was getting disgusted with this too, for nothing seemed to be working. On one of my visits to the doctor, he examined me only to find that I was already pregnant. I wish I could say that I never waivered, because I did. The only thing I could do is say, Lord, I believe; help my unbelief. In spite of my wavering, God through his grace and mercy touched my body and I conceived our second son, Exh. Matthew David Watson.

Satan was not satisfied: During the first three months of my pregnancy, I experienced intense pain and suffering. I thought I was going to have a miscarriage. Fibroid tumors were enlarging, along with the fetus in my uterus and causing the intense pain. I could barely eat anything. I would go to noon day prayer and would be so sick that I would just lay across the bench and pray. One night Bishop came by our apartment with another minister from the Pool. I was upstairs lying down and Eld. Watson was down stairs with little Gary. When I heard Bishop's voice, I immediately came down to greet him. We did not stay too long, but just as he was leaving we were standing at the door and Bishop said "I think Sis Harriet needs prayer before we leave." Bishop prayed and then quickly left. A month later, this was my third month of pregnancy, and I would have this intense pain normally at the time that my monthly cycle would begin. Satan was trying to make me miscarry. When the time came, I looked for the pain that I had previously experienced in that two months prior to this, but there was none! God healed me through the prayer of Bishop White! I delivered a healthy baby boy at the right time!

No room in the inn: The Lord had healed my body and enabled me to conceive again about a year later. At this time we were living in a two-bedroom apartment. Gary Jr. shared a bedroom with Matthew. I was currently pregnant with Nicholas. We needed a place to live, but at that time we did not have money for a down payment on a house. Bishop had been preaching that the young couples needed to get out of these apartments into a house. We needed to stop adding up rent receipts and get houses so the young couples could begin to have something other than rent receipts. At this time the City of Columbus came up with the Dollar House Program. The city provided a select group of houses. Applicants could submit their name to a list for each house that they desired to have. Applicant names would be put in a container for each house available to be purchased. Time and time again we would put our names in for houses, but we never were selected. Although, almost at each lottery someone from our church would win a house. It was said that the Pool of Bethesda seemed to have a **"Inside Track"** for being selected to win a house. But it was God honoring Bishop White's words of wisdom to the young couples. We still had not won a house. I told Bro. Watson, after one evening of going and not winning a house, that I was not going to have faith for a house anymore, he could have all the faith. I was angry with the Lord! Boy, did I have nerve! Elder Watson encouraged me and told me that we had to keep on believing the Lord. I told him that he could keep believing if he wanted to. I was like Job's wife for a moment. Little did I know that the Lord was teaching me a lesson. After time passed, it was getting near my delivery time and we were still in a two bedroom apartment. One day, one of the brothers at the church told Eld. Watson and I that Bishop had been praying for us and said that we were going to get a house in the Dollar House Lottery coming up. I remember that day like it was yesterday. It was like Tuesday night, like many Tuesday nights when the city would have the Dollar House Lottery. Eld. Watson and I would come back and the saints would ask us had we won a house. We would always have to say no. So here we were at another Tuesday – the Dollar House Lottery. We arrived late that night, and the lottery was being held on the Riverfront. After we parked the car and began to walk across the field to the bleachers, I heard the announcer say Gary. I listened closely, I was running at this time, I knew that there were a lot of Garys but very few of them have Harriets. So they said Gary and Harriet Watson. I began to run even faster. When I got to the stage, I was out of breath. I was pregnant and grinning from ear to ear. I had gotten to the podium first, and finally Elder Watson and Gary Jr. walked up too. They too, were grinning. The news media was there. They took a picture of us and the picture was in the Columbus Dispatch Newspaper. The article reported that so many houses had been won by our members in our church. This Tuesday, we were going back with a good report. Our names not only had been called for one house, but three houses. Bishop said that our names would really be in the lottery. In other words, our names would be called for more than one house. Although we had to choose the first house our name was called for, the house we were called for was the one that we wanted. It is not just the house I was glad about, but God taught me a lesson. If I had won the house when I thought we should have won the house, I would have gotten all caught up in it. But the Lord through his grace and mercy, held back His blessing until I could receive it with the right attitude. He also taught me to be happy when others were being blessed, and there is always an appointed time. It also taught me to keep "material things" in their proper place and never let them affect how I feel towards God. It is not good to get caught up in material things. I thank God for his love and his teaching.

THESE ARE THEY WHICH RECEIVED MIRACLES WHILE ATTENDING THE POOL OF BETHESDA, CLGI

FROM 1977-1993

DANIEL GOINS: Daniel Goins was playing in the garage with his brother. They found a can of gasoline and decided to investigate it. Some of the gasoline spilled on his clothing. The children lit a match and immediately Daniel became a ball of fire. The child was severely burned on his face arms and chest. Bishop White was called. He laid his hands on him and prayed the prayer of faith. Daniel began to recover quickly and his burns began to peel and heal. This was a miracle, instead of being scarred for life, Daniel Goins' skin returned to normal and he is well today!

JOYCE HOLMES (Mason-Haile): Joyce Holmes had a severe problem with perspiration and decided to have surgery on her underarms. The surgery was not a success on one of her arms. There was a large hole under her arm and it wouldn't heal. One night in service Bishop White told all those that were ill to come by the organ and he would lay hands on them. The next day, Joyce looked under her arm and the Lord had put a layer of skin over the opening, it was truly a miracle. Joyce immediately went over to Bishop White's home to show him what the Lord had done. As of this day, Joyce Holmes still has her miracle, not only did God put a layer of skin over the hole, but she does not sweat or have any odor under that arm.

Also, Joyce was scheduled for surgery on Tuesday for a diagnosis of cancer, and requested prayer on Sunday. At the pre-surgery check, the doctors found no trace of the disease. No explanation on the surgeon's part could be given.

DARRELL CELLER: Darrell Celler, eleven years old, was healed miraculously of asthma. This condition existed from birth and nearly resulted in the loss of life.

JESSIE HOPE: Sister Hope experienced symptoms of a heart attack and was rushed to the hospital. On Thursday, upon hearing of this, Bishop White declared by faith that it was not so. She was released with a clean bill of health.

GWAIN BRACY: Broth Gwain suffered from youth with Asthma, he was known at the local hospitals as a regular emergency case. One evening before service began, the symptoms of a severe attack occurred. Bishop White and the saints prayed and God delivered him that very evening. He has been completely free ever since.

TOMMISENA KAMBON (Hall): Tommisena Kambon had a problem with her shoulder; it would slip out of socket from time to time. She had surgery on it, but the problem continued. During our Christian Education picnic, she pulled her shoulder out of socket again, and was rushed to the hospital. The next day during service, Bishop White called her up to the organ and laid his hands on her and began to pray. Tommisena began to scream, the power of God shot through her shoulder and it jumped back into place. The power of God was so strong that it frightened Tommisena,

but as of this day, her shoulder has never jumped out of place again.

ANNIE RUFFIN: Annie Ruffin broke her wrist and was wearing a cast. During a Sunday morning service, Bishop White told her to come up for prayer. Bishop White began to pray and her cast began to get really warm. After prayer, the swelling and pain left her arm and the cast became loose. She returned to her doctor and he took x-rays and found that the bones were no longer broken, but perfect.

ROBERTA PEYTON: Roberta Peyton was pregnant with Justin. About the 3rd month of pregnancy the baby stopped moving and growing. The doctor said he was dead. Bishop White called Roberta to the prayer line and began to ask God to give life back to this baby. In three days' time, Roberta's stomach began to grow twice as fast and the baby began to kick and move. What a MIRACLE! Justin was born healthy and was very smart.

PATRICIA CAMPBELL: Patricia Campbell's baby died in her womb due to carbon monoxide poisoning. She came up for prayer and God brought that baby back to life and he had no type of birth defect because of the poison that was ingested in his system. At one time the doctor said he may have some mental problems, but he was healthy and very alert.

DOREEN DOBSON: When Doreen came to the Pool of Bethesda, she had a severe back problem and a very weak heart. After attending the Pool and becoming saved and called to the ministry. God performed several miracles in her body. Not only did God heal her from all the pain, He gave her a brand new heart.

KATHY PRICE: Kathy Price was admitted in the middle of the night, she had a terrible bowel obstruction and the doctors thought they would have to cut some of her intestines. However, Bishop White was called and he began to pray. Kathy had surgery, but when they went in, they found that it was not necessary to a take portion of her intestine out. Kathy began to heal immediately and as you know a deep incision takes at least six weeks or longer to heal. Kathy's incision began to heal immediately and when she went back to the doctor, he was shocked because the womb was healed completely. He told her to leave his office and not to come back because she told him that God had healed her.

HARRIET CAREY (Harriet Watson's Mother, healing by proxy): Mrs. Carey had kidney stones and was scheduled for surgery. Elder Harriet Watson requested prayer and Bishop White remembered her at the end of service. When the doctors begin to prepare her for surgery, they checked her again and this time, the KIDNEY STONE HAD DISAPPEARED. God is GREAT. The surgery naturally was cancelled.

TOMMI MOORE: Surgery for reconstruction for his kidney and bladder. The doctors had decided that Tommie would have to have an Ostomy bag, his mother, Elder Meta Chube requested prayer and Bishop began to pray and lay hands on him. Elder Chube asked the doctors to check again before they proceeded with the surgery, they found absolutely NO DAMAGE TO THE KIDNEY OR BLADDER. What a MIGHTY GOD WE SERVE. Naturally the surgery was cancelled, leaving the doctors speechless.

KIM MCMILLON: Kim McMillon was a young girl and had been in the church all of her life. Her mother, Louise McMillon was in the medical field and discovered a mole on Kim's back. The mole looked really strange, so her mother took her to a doctor where the area was tested and diagnosed as cancer. The whole family was devastated. They called Bishop White immediately. Kim got into every prayer line from then on and Bishop would lay hands on her. When it was time for her next doctor's appointment, the doctors saw a change in her mole. They tested it and again and it was no longer CANCER. THIS IS TRULY THE POWER OF GOD. As of this day, cancer has not reoccurred.

DOUG MCMILLON: Doug McMillon is Kim's younger brother. Doug was hit by a car when he was very young. He was so severely injured that he was put into an entire body cast. They almost lost him, but God stepped in, through prayer. He is fine today.

RON & SHEILA FLEMING: While Sheila was pregnant her baby Stephen had stopped moving. The doctor's couldn't find any type of movement and said, "He was dead". Sheila came up for prayer and GOD REVERSED THE DECISION. Stephen is now close to six feet tall and healthy.

ONE HUNDREDFOLD FINANCIAL AND MATERIAL MIRACLES

3 John 1:2

Behold, I wish above all things that thou mayest prosper and be in health even as thy soul prospereth.

MECHANICAL, FINANCIAL, SICKNESS, DEATH AND FAMILY

Min. Josephine Clark, Pool of Bethesda CLGI, Midwest Jurisdiction

For the past 20 years, God has been moving mightily in my life through the prayers of Bishop Joseph White. I have seen miracle after miracle, mechanical, financial, sickness, death and family.

Just recently, I was having a problem with my automobile, and I did not know what to do, other than take it to the dealer. But, during Friday night service, the Bishop asked those who needed God to move for them to stand out in the aisle. I stood out and the next morning my automobile problem was solved. My hospital and doctor bills were paid, when the insurance company said they would not pay, after prayer God moved and changed the hearts of the insurance company representatives and the bills were paid. After my divorce, the mortgage company was going to foreclose on my home, after prayer everything was taken care of, and I have been able to pay off the mortgage. I have been healed many times from viruses and the flu. One time in particular, about two years ago while coming home from Belpre, Ohio. I began to shiver and my teeth were chattering. When I got home, it seemed like I was going to freeze to death. I asked my children to request prayer for me when they went to church, and at around 10:00 that night, my fever broke and I was able to get up and eat. When they came home, they told me that the Bishop and the church had prayed for me. When my mother, my brother, and two sisters passed away over the years, God has taken me through, and given me peace in every situation. I have been able to raise my four children from the ages of 1, 8, 9 and 10 to the ages of 17, 25, 26 and 27 in this Gospel, by the grace of God and through the prayers of Bishop Joseph White.

Min. Ron Talley, Pool of Bethesda, Midwest Jurisdiction

Sunday morning, December18, 1994, Bishop preached on the account when Jesus turned water into wine. He gave us specific instructions as we gave our offering.

Before this point, I had recently left my job without having one to go to. In September, two weeks before the Missionary conference, I put in weeks notice and did not tell anyone. I was stepping out on faith. The Lord was showing me in different ways that He was going to move for me. It was a difficult decision for me to leave a job not knowing where the next job was. The month of September was hard to bare on the job, the devil really performed. I know now how the Lord was teaching me to trust in Him. I gave notice and my supervisor was shocked, but I felt a release. I did not tell anyone.

I did not want to face the opinions. I knew it was my turn to trust in the Lord for myself. I knew some would come to in agreement, wanting to understand, trying to share in my hurt. But there was no hurt, I knew it would be hard for me to explain my step of faith. This step, was the direction and the tone by which my existence in Christ would be established. The devil's thoughts of my decision was obvious, I did not want anyone to suffer temptation, therefore I told no one.

My last week of work happened to be the week of the Missionary Conference. I was not going. I planned to use that time to find a job. I wanted to have a great testimony real soon. There was a certain prophet who during the month of September would ask me if I was going to the convention. I would always tell her, "I do not think so". She would say "The Lord will make a way." It was the week of the convention, I knew I was not going, it was my last week at work, and I was going to find a job. Then that Wednesday night, a pastor called me, wanting to help him drive to Fort Walton Beach, Florida. He planned to depart that same evening. I only had two days left to work, and thought, "I have no job." I told him I probably could not get the time off. He said, "Call and find out." Trying to be obedient I said, "Yes". I sat there on the bed thinking, it was around 9:00 pm and the pastor was leaving a midnight. I just sat there thinking how could I leave now? I had no job, little money and bills to be paid. I called the pastor back and told him I would not be able to go. He said, "Did you ask?" I remained quiet; I did not want to lie. I said, "I will call you back." I called my supervisor, but the manager answered the phone. I could not believe it, so I told her about the conference and that a pastor wanted me to help drive to Fort Walton Beach. The manager told me that it was ok and that I could get my things later. Then I talked to the supervisor, she had no problem with it. I called the pastor and said, "Well what time do you want me at your house?"

We arrived at the conference on Thursday, got up early Friday morning and went to the beach and stayed there for at least eight hours. It was a blessing. Friday morning, I used the pay phone to call back home to Ohio, checking on an application I had delivered early that week, nothing came of it. There was a sister who asked me, "Who I was calling?" For the first time, I shared some of the events, she said, "The Lord will make a way".

It was time for Friday night service, Bishop White, was ministering and he called several people to stand in the aisle, then he called me to step out. He said, "I don't know what you are going through, but the Lord wants you to know that you have made the right decision." I think that was the first time Bishop said anything to me during the service. You know when the man of God is calling others to stand in the aisle, and you are asking the Lord, please, have him call my name. I needed to hear from God, this was setting the tone of my walk in Christ. Finding a job that weekend, could not have given me the joy and the blessed assurance I received that night.

I told it all, this paper could easily be a book. Let's get to the "Draw out your blessing sermon." Bishop was preaching from this account when Jesus turned water into wine, His first miracle. They poured in water, but drew out wine. Bishop told us when we give our offering to say, "Offering I put in, Blessing I draw out." Let me interject this piece of information, the Lord sent me to work through a temporary service, for a corporation I tried to get into back in 1990, before I was saved. I knew it was the Lord, because it was Sunday night after youth service, a lady from the temporary agency called, asking if I would want to work for this particular corporation. I said, "Yes". She told me when I arrive in the morning, to ask for Joy. I said, "Ask for who?" She said, the ladies' name is Joy. I said OK, when I get off the phone I cried and shouted in my room.

Back to the sermon of December 18, 1994. I put in my offering and drew out a full time position on December 19, 1994, it was 3:00 pm when the human resources made me an offer. My God is a good God, and his servant Bishop Joseph White is worthy to be honored. That December 19, 1994 blessing increased my income by $4,008. On January 24, 1996, I received a promotion that was a increase of $3,532. On December 18, 1994, I put in $10.00 and drew out an annual increase of $7,540 as of January 24, 1996. That is the only a period of 1 year 1 month and 7 days. On February 1998, my pay increased $3,500, and during July 1998, I received another promotion with an increase of another $3000.

Min. Patricia Ingle, Pool of Bethesda CLG, Midwest Jurisdiction

I praise God, for Jesus is help in trouble and peril. Some years ago I was driving to work on a cold, snowy, icy, wintery morning. I was on the freeway going south to downtown Columbus. Upon approaching a curve, my car slid all the way across the right lane to the center lane. My car started to spin, hitting the cement road divider, and I was facing oncoming traffic. I was terrified expecting a head on collision but God touched the car and gently turned it. The car finally stopped. I was no longer facing oncoming traffic, but my car ended up in a lane where there was no moving traffic. The miracle of it all, was I not turned in the right direction. My car was not damaged, no dents, or parts hanging/missing. It was as if a wall of protection was around me. I was not injured, did not have a scratch, bruise, cut or nose bleed. I did not bump my head, or slam my hands or body against the steering wheel or interior of the car. Praise God, the Lord makest us to swell in safety. I'm so glad that I belong in a ministry that teaches us the word and how to pray, for truly I was depending on both.

Mins. Barbara & Joseph Johnson, Pool of Bethesda CLG, Midwest Jurisdiction

We want to thank and praise the Lord for all of his miracles in our lives, truly saving our sin sick souls was a miracle. But God didn't just stop there. When my family came to the Lord we had a nickel to our names, literally a nickel. But the joy of the Lord filled us and so changed our lives that we were rich with his grace.

Little did we know that one day when the world tried to keep it from us, the Lord blessed us with the RICHES OF ABRAHAM, $44,000.00 and today we watch as our first home is being built.

God has and continues to bless us. Saints, we love the Lord with all of our hearts and souls. And if that house was to go and the money would run out, it would never make us turn around because the biggest miracle was saving our sick sin souls.

Elder Sharon Alston, International Director of Missions, Pool of Bethesda CLG, Midwest Jurisdiction

God has done so much for me in these last 20 years, it would take a book to tell of his goodness, however, I just want to share a few things with you. Through the prayers and faithfulness of my Pastor, Bishop Joseph White, God has given me a brand new life.

When I first came to the Pool of Bethesda, God started working on me immediately through the word. I received Salvation, then the process of deprogramming from an occult religious background started. Along with this, deliverance came from the spirit of suicide, hatred, bitterness, mistrust, and unbelief, then the Lord really began to touch me and started mending my broken heart.

The Lord has blessed me materially, and I have never had a furniture bill. God has always provided me with new furniture and new cars. I can say that these years with God have been the most prosperous and uplifting years that anyone could experience.

The Lord changed me totally and made me into a usable vessel for this ministry. God has taken me all over the world to preach his gospel and has truly brought a GREAT TRANSFORMATION to me.

Thank you Bishop for all your time, prayers, teaching and faithfulness. You have been my prime example of how to serve the True and Living God.

Sister Juliann and Randy Bryant, Bethesda CLG, Midwest Jurisdiction

We were all blessed when my Sis. Juliann and her husband Randy Bryant came back to the church. They received the Lord in their lives to increase everyone's faith, Pastor Battee spoke a word of faith. She said the Lord was going to bless Randy with a job and when he got home, the phone is going to ring or there would be a message on the answer machine. Our Mighty God did just that! He received a call and the job started the same week. Not only was he blessed with a job, but Rev. Shelly Battee and also Sis. Michelle Battee were also in the same week. Elder Lisa was also blessed with a raise after only working there for 6 months. What a blessing! What a miracle!!

Elder Shirley Bailey, Trinity CLG, Midwest Jurisdiction

In Feb. of 1994, I was able to purchase my home. It was a dollar home but it was not in the Ohio Dollar Home Lottery. It was in probate court. When I went to the lottery for the home all the homes were taken. I just resolved in myself that I would have a home in Heaven, because I would never, first of all financially, be able to get one and second, that was the last year they would have the dollar house program. But, a few months later, the city called me and told me to my pull my name out of the files and asked if I wanted a dollar house. I thought they were pulling a prank or it was a mistake, but it wasn't. The Lord gave me my house, allowed my financial situation not to stop me from getting the loan to renovate, and gave me a mortgage lower than the rent I was paying. Everything worked out for my good and it was nobody but the Lord, he gave me a financial miracle.

Elder Sister Gladys Calix-Ferguson, Asst Pastor, New Jerusalem, Croughton, UK, Church of the Living God Bible Study, London, UK

As most of the members of the Church of the Living God know, Bishop White has prophesied and prayed for the ministry in London. One year after the Lord first put it on Bishop's heart to pray for me in my work in London, we have a building, which contains all the microphones, all speakers, drums, chairs, kitchen, fellowship annex and is only one block from my apartment! Praise his holy name!

Every week we have service and every week different people drop in off the streets. The saints in the UK support the work in London with their time, traveling down to be there for the service. Be encouraged! The Lord is moving. On a personal side, I had never experienced the Lord's power directly. In October 1996, Bishop White turned and looked at me in the middle of his sermon and told me not to sell my apartment and that the Lord would bless me to be able to keep it and would increase my financial blessings.

I was obedient and did not sell and waited. The Lord made a way for me to go back to London easily. I give God the glory and testify that in February 1999, due to my obedience to the man of God, and the Lord's power and Spirit moving through him, I received word from the lawyers that I was given the apartment, plus a considerable sum. I will now have a profit on the property and we have a church around the corner from there!

GLORY BE TO GOD AND OUR WONDERFUL SAVIOR. GOD BLESS YOU ALWAYS BISHOP WHITE.

THE WATER IS TROUBLED AT THE POOL OF BETHESDA CHURCH OF THE LIVING GOD INTERNATIONAL

In 1978 the State of Ohio introduced a Dollar Home purchasing lottery. The homes were purchased for one dollar and it was your responsibility to secure financing to renovate. The saints at the Pool of Bethesda were truly blessed by this program. Through the prayers and faith of Bishop White, the following won houses, and today the majority have resold these homes and gone on to bigger and better homes.

DOLLAR HOUSES WON THROUGH THE PRAYERS OF BISHOP JOSEPH WHITE.

First dollar house was won by Ann and Charles Leister 4/78.

Carolin Howard Taylor won the 2nd 6/78

Sister Elizabeth Murphy won the 3rd 10/78

Afterwards 24 others won homes between 1979 and 1981.

Robert and carol Shelton

Joyce Haile

Mary Bracy

Charles and Wilda Johnson

Lance and Lorain Gibson

Marvin and Lynett McIntye

Ronnie and Sheila Fleming

Jackie and Nate Goins

Daryl and Karen Hampton

Gary & Harriet Watson

Brother & Sister Pritchard

Sister Dot Bracy

BOOK OF MIRACLES: SECOND EDITION MARCH 2014

A Quick Visit

Miracle for Sister Shaquira Speaks, New and Living Way, Pastor Kevin Glover (SEJ)

Healing of Cyst from Ovaries

I had been having very bad menstrual cramps since I was 10 years old. I would just crawl in the bed and curl up because my cramps were so severe. I would have to take 800 mg Ibuprofen for relief. The pain was so unbearable that I finally asked my mom to take me to the doctor. She took me to have an ultrasound, and they found cysts on my ovaries. During my menstrual cycle, the cysts would enlarge and cause me severe pain. One weekday, Dr. Crystal Lucky came through for a quick visit, and after she preached, she called a prayer line. When she prayed for me, she prophesied that the Lord was going to do something for me. I went back for my follow-up with the Obstetrician. The doctor did a second ultra-sound, found that all of the cysts were gone, and I have not been in pain since. (submitted 2012)

The Lord is Faithful by Min. Yasmine Robinson

About two and a half years ago, I develop a cyst on my left hand. Over the course of time, the cyst continued to grow and caused me much discomfort and pain. As the cyst increased, so did the numbness and tingling sensation which greatly concerned me. As time passed, my writing became impaired and normal day to day activities such as typing or holding my bible became increasingly difficult in so much that my nine year old daughter, Jada, had begun taking notes on my behalf; as I was unable to properly grip my pen.

It was then that I decided to see a hand specialist who informed me that the cyst was pressing on a nerve and recommend surgery. After much prayer and consideration, I elected to have surgery in March of 2011. A week after the surgery, the cyst grew back larger than it was before. Despite an overwhelming sense of discouragement, I continued to pray because I had no other options but the Lord. I began to recall all of the healing testimonies of the saints. I started to pray from the various healing accounts that the Lord performed in the Bible. Service after service I asked the Lord to remember me. Prayer line after prayer line, I stood in hope of the Lord's grace and eventually he responded.

April 9, 2011, Sis. Vanita Brunson graciously drove me up to Philadelphia to run a Missions Revival at Sword of the Spirit, but it was there that the Lord would revive me. I rode to Philadelphia in pain, wondering how I was going to make it through the weekend. Due to the weather, we arrived mid way through the testimony service, but just in time to hear the testimony of Min. Melissa Webb. Min. Webb testified of how the Lord healed her of pre-cancerous cells that were found on her cervix. As she testified, it increased my faith, but not only my faith, the faith of everyone in the building. The Spirit fell during the testimony service and everyone began to magnify the Lord. As I lifted my left hand in worship, the Holy Spirit encouraged me to open my eyes. He said, "Look at your hand". I watched in amazement as the cyst began to dissolve before my very eyes. I could not believe it. I felt like the leaper who was not only cleansed but made whole.

The evening of April 9, 2011 the prayers of the righteous did avail.

Brandon White

Three years ago, the Lord healed me from a disease I suffered from for fourteen years called congestive heart failure or CHF. When I was twelve years old I frequently visited the hospital because I was not feeling well, but doctors never knew what was wrong with me. After several months of testing, the doctors finally diagnosed me with congestive heart failure(CHF). I was diagnosed with this disease because the muscles of my heart were extremely hard; it was not pumping enough blood, and one of the ventricles or chambers on the left side of my heart were separating. These complications were caused by the fluid constricting my heart. At the time, the doctors thought it was caused by cancer, so at the age of twelve I went through my first treatment of chemotherapy and had fluid drained from my lungs.

As I got older, my condition started to worsen. From ages fourteen to sixteen, doctors were putting oxygen in my blood because there was not enough oxygen going from my heart to the other organs in my body. This caused my heart rate and blood pressure to drop frequently, my feet and legs to swell, and it was hard to sleep during the night. From ages seventeen to nineteen, I consumed almost twenty pills a day just to stay alive and had a strict diet to follow.

For ten years, I was told every two weeks by doctors that I was going to die. At age seventeen the doctors performed an angioplasty, a procedure that widens narrowed arteries, because I was being placed on dialysis. The doctors put a tube in my arm and my groin to make it easier to retrieve blood from me if need be. The angioplasty caused a blood clot to form in my heart forcing the doctors to do a bypass surgery to try and remove it. After I had all these procedures done, they still could not heal me. At the age of nineteen, I had another angioplasty done. After the surgery, the doctors were still unable to fix the problem so they added more pills to my daily regiment.

The doctors told me that my heart was aging faster than the rest of my body, and when I was twenty-one I had my first heart attack. I had another bypass surgery done. The doctors performed the surgery by going in through my armpit and down my side because I had so much fluid on my heart that they were afraid of collapsing my lungs. The doctors said that I had a mild heart attack, and had been having mini heart attacks for months. I received some additional pills. At the age of twenty-three, I had my second heart attack. After this heart attack the doctors performed a surgery on me every week. This resulted in more testing and more doctors cutting on me. I was sent to UCLA and USC to see if there was anything else that could be done for me. After the doctors there tested me and figured out that there was nothing else that could be done, they transferred me to Baylor University. The doctors ran more tests on me, increased my pill consumption, and in addition to that, I had more chemotherapy treatments and dialysis done.

The CHF had become more aggressive. My kidneys and lungs began to fail and my heart rate began to drop as low as six beats per minute. During this time I was visiting the hospital everyday receiving chemotherapy treatments, dialysis and having numerous tests performed on me. This continued until the age of twenty-six.

In 2010, I was told that there was nothing else that could be done for me and I had twelve hours to live. That very same day the man of God, Bishop White, was in town running a revival at El Paso Worship Center. I was invited to this revival and decided to attend. At the end of his sermon, he called a prayer line and asked me to come down. He told me that the Lord wanted to do something for me. Bishop White had no idea what I was going through or even who I was. Bishop White began to pray and he said, "Loose him. Loose him. Loose him." Something went through me, and at that time I did not know what it was. After learning more about this Gospel, I now know it was the Holy Ghost. I was healed immediately! The next day I went to the hospital and the doctors were surprised to see me walk in. They proceeded on with their routine testing and found nothing. All the fluid around my heart was gone. I do not take any pills, I am not receiving chemotherapy treatments or dialysis and by the grace of God I am here today; I can share my testimony with all of you. Glory to God!!

Bro. Clark Billingsley Jr's Healing Testimony

I thank God and his son Jesus to be able to give this healing testimony, and the Holy Spirit for keeping me through it all.

Over the course of a year, dating back to December 2011, I began experiencing episodes of brief unconsciousness with no awareness of my surroundings. It became so severe that I sustained a head injury and tore several tendons in my shoulder and wrist. I also lost consciousness while driving, but I thank the Lord I was able to pull over to the side of the road.

During this time, I was restricted from driving for seven months. The doctors were trying to find a diagnosis for my condition and provide a remedy to prevent it from occurring again. I was referred to a neurologist, a cardiologist and underwent numerous MRIs and CT-scans. The doctors found a cyst located between my brain and spinal cord, but could not be positive that it was causing my episodes of unconsciousness. There was a possibility that I might have to live with this condition and driving restrictions for the rest of my life. I was prescribed several different medications with strong side effects that were hard on my body and mind, but God had the Holy Spirit within me doing a mighty work.

I knew what the doctors told me about my condition, but I never lost faith in the Lord and trusted him with my life. I knew that without God the Father, Jesus and the Holy Spirit, I simply would not be able to deal with this by myself. Throughout this whole situation I prayed; my family, the elders and saints of the Church of the Living God International continued to keep me uplifted in prayer for a healing in my body.

God healed my sick body. It was just a matter of keeping faith in God and letting the power of the Holy Spirit continue to work inside me. Over time, an awesome miracle of the Lord Jesus Christ was revealed and witnessed. There are no more episodes of unconsciousness and I am able to drive without any restrictions. I went from taking several different medications to now, just one daily. My cyst has not grown any larger since it was discovered.

The Lord can do amazing things if we continue to have faith and let the Holy Spirit guide us. Jesus came to die on the cross to save us from our sins. That is how much he loves us. He will never leave you, even in your darkest hour. I am a walking, breathing miracle of what our Lord, God, has done. I am healed and I thank God the Father, his son Jesus Christ and the Holy Spirit.

DAVID WATERS

BETHEL CLGI -GW JURISDICTION

I was on my way to work and I had an accident. I was going around a curve and I hit a patch of ice. I spun out of control and landed on an embankment of a pond. The top of the pond was frozen. The car broke the top layer of ice, but did not go any further than the embankment. I'm doing fine. The Lord really kept me. I was sitting in the back of one of the cop cars. I was talking with the officer and she informed me that in these types of accidents, my car should have flipped over and landed roof down in the pond. I am glad that I serve the Lord. It was the multitude of God's tender mercies that kept me that day. I praise Him for it because God is just so good, he did not have to keep me, but I am glad that He did.

CHAVALA CHAMPION, ETERNAL LIFE CLGI - SE JURISDICTION

In 2004 my daughter, Haley C. Henry, was three years old. Since birth she has had respiratory problems, a case of apnea, and was diagnosed with chronic asthma at age 1. Haley had been hospitalized twice. We started visiting Eternal Life in Columbus, GA in February and in June we became members. In August, the church laid hands on Haley and we prayed that the Lord would touch her and take the sickness from her body. On August 19, 2004, I took Haley to her physical at Dr. Panvelkar's office and they did a complete physical examination on her. Dr. Panvelkar stated that we were taking Haley off the nebulizer machine and steroids. At the time, Haley was taking 3 to 4 different medications daily. We were advised to give her only Singulair once every night. My daughter was delivered from asthma. The Lord healed her and increased our faith in God and in that City.

Death Stops and Life Starts

Elder Francine Roach, Pastor, Restoration, Columbia, SC (SEJ), 5 February 2012

Praise the Lord. I would like to thank God for his healing power. I would also like to thank God for Bishop White, a man of faith and power. In October 1999, I was diagnosed with breast cancer. When you hear about cancer, of course, death is the first thing that comes to mind. The end of October at the Midwest Jurisdictional Meeting, and again at the Brotherhood Meeting in November, Bishop White was preaching about life being present through the Holy Ghost. At both of these meetings, Bishop White and the seasoned saints of the Pool of Bethesda, who have seen the many miracles, prayed for me. Also, Bishop Edwards had encouraged me that God could stop the spread of cancer in my body.

Later in November, I had to have surgery and they removed three tumors and thirty lymph nodes. Seven of the lymph nodes were positive for cancer meaning the cancer should have and could have spread to other parts of my body. Ten years later, in 2009, during my annual mammogram my left breast had the same type of calcification that was detected in 1999. But what should have been cancer is not. Why, you ask? Because the miracle working power of God stopped the spread of cancer in my body by the power of the Holy Ghost that lives in me. It is 2012, and I am still cancer free.

EBONY CORNISH

COLUMBIA, SC

On Friday night, during the General Assembly, Bishop White prayed for Ebony's baby. Although, she was looking for a miracle that could only be seen on the ultrasound, God gave her a visible miracle the next morning. While Bishop White was praying for her, he asked her three times was the baby growing. According to the doctor, the baby was growing normally; God saw different. The next day we saw a notable miracle; her stomach had grown bigger. When she returned home from the General Assembly, people saw the difference. A week before the General Assembly Ebony interviewed for a job. The lady that conducted the interview saw her after the General Assembly and said, “I had no idea you were pregnant.” One of her closest friends was so amazed when she saw her; she asked, “How did you get so big so fast?” That was a miracle. We go to the doctor on June 22 and are expecting to see another miracle on the ultrasound. Praise God! I have submitted the before and after pictures. (Submitted 2012)

Don’t Worry…Go Believing!

Ms. Lula Matthews, Grandmother, of Sis Nardia Matthews

Augusta Worship Center, Pastor Jay Johnson

My grandmother started having unbearable pains on the left side of her neck. On a scale of one to ten, she ranked the pain past a ten. To get temporary relief, she put hot packs on her neck. In February, she went to the doctor about the pain. He performed a series of tests on her because he believed she may have thyroid cancer. This diagnosis came right as Elder Alston was passing through the land. My grandmother’s test came back negative, but the pain persisted. At my request, my grandmother came to Elder Alston’s revival. Elder Alston laid hands on my grandmother, told her not to worry that everything was going to be alright, the Lord was healing her body, and to go believing. After Elder Alston prayed for my grandmother, she stated her pain had decreased and now her pain could be ranked as a six.

In March, she had regular follow-ups with the doctor. Eventually, the doctor explained to her she needed to see a thyroid specialist because he still believed she had cancer. In April, the specialist called her back for her final appointment. The doctor walked into the room, looked at my grandma and said, "Ms. Matthews tell me what is wrong with you?" My grandma responded, "I don't know you tell me, that's what I'm here to see you for." After a brief uneasy laugh, the doctor told her, "Well, Ms. Matthews, there is nothing wrong with you. There is no cancer! The test results we have here show nothing there. The only thing I can say is, you need a good one hour massage." I myself was unaware that she was going to the doctor to be tested for cancer. The Lord is so good. My grandmother is not a member of Augusta Worship Center. But I do know that because of the words that the Holy Spirit gave to Elder Alston to speak to my grandma, she believed, and through her faith she was healed.

Calling On Jesus, by Joseph Quattlebum

On a fall day in 1999, our family went to the park for the kids to play. Joseph was about four years old and had a fever the day before, but he was feeling better this day. The kids finished eating McDonalds, and were running around playing. We were getting ready to leave the park, when Mark and I heard a clicking noise. We thought that Joe was playing around, but when we turned to look at him his eyes were rolling in the back of head and he was making the clicking noise. Mark jerked the car in park and jumped out to grab Joe; he was not breathing or responding. Mark was attempting to do CPR but it was not working, so he started calling on Jesus. I walked away because I did not want to be over emotional while Mark was trying to get him to breath. All the while, Mark was calling on Jesus.

There was a group of people that just came from a CPR class and they stopped to assist Mark. So many people were calling the ambulance that they arrived in less than two or three minutes. When paramedics arrived, Joe was still unresponsive, but the clicking had stopped. The paramedics woke Joe up, but he was not talking and looked space out. I was panicking by this time, and Mark was still praying and calling on Jesus. Joe became fully conscious and vomited up pieces of french-fries that he had prior to the attack. The paramedics said that he had a seizure due to his high fever. They also informed me that when he vomited there was a risk of him choking, but God kept him.

The paramedics put Joe into the ambulance. I rode with him and Mark and our other son, Stephen, followed behind in the car. Joe was beginning to speak, but he was not forming his words correctly. His words sounded like when a baby first recognizes that they have a voice. I began to panic even the more. The paramedic was talking to Joe; looking for him to respond, but he was still having trouble forming his words. I would call his name, but still the same results. The paramedic told me, because he was unconscious and without oxygen for over five minutes, it could have caused brain damage. There was a possibility that I might have to teach him how to talk and walk all over again. That was not the news I wanted to hear. Joe was looking at me and I could see he wanted to say mom, but still no words. I started praying and calling on Jesus.

We arrived at the hospital, and Joe was still struggling to speak. Mark called the saints at the Pool of Bethesda to pray for Joe. We believe the saints were praying for him immediately. Why, you ask? While Mark was asking the saints to pray, I was with Joe trying to get him to say mommy. I laid my hands on his head and said, "**JESUS!**" The prayers of the righteous saints availed much. Joe was trying to say words, but they were not coming out like words. My God, who is a miracle worker, began to touch Joe's speech and he was pushing out the word "mommy". Then, he said it more and more. God was moving by His Spirit in front of my eyes. When the doctor says one thing, God says another. Jesus, who has all power to touch the brain that was without oxygen for over five minutes and bring life to that, which should have been dead. Life was brought back to Joe and he was able to speak again. He was even able to sit up so that the doctor could check his breathing. We still do not have a definite reason for the episode, but God who gave His only begotten son allowed us the ability to call on Jesus. If you call on his name you shall be saved. Today, Joe does not have any of the complications from this episode; God has called him into the ministry, and he has answered the call. Praise God for allowing us to call on Jesus.

MIRACLES AND HEALINGS

ELDER CRAIG BLACK

SWORD OF THE SPIRIT, CLGI, PHILADELPHIA, PA

I have been paralyzed, confided to a wheelchair, due to a car accident since May 14, 1981. From that time until the year 2002 I had at least one major surgery every year, various hospitals stays for various ailments, many emergency visits, and blood transfusions. Suffering through all these medical conditions brought me to a point where I just settled in this life of detrimental health issues.

One year I grew frustrated on how these health issues where limiting me in the ministry. I started asking Bishop White and the saints to pray for me regarding these matters. Bishop White not only prayed for me consistently, but he sent me the following scripture regularly – Proverbs 3:8- via email. When Bishop Edwards preached, she would call me down for prayer every meeting that I attended. She too would send me scripture to pray and live by; that began to build my faith in knowing that I having to go through surgeries, hospital stays, emergency visits and blood transfusions did not have to be my life in Christ Jesus.

As a result of the Lord's power, mercy, grace and hearing of their prayers, my testimony is that since the year 2002 I have not had one surgery, no emergency room visits, no hospital stays and no more blood transfusion. Now that is mixing the word with faith and having to see the manifestation of faith working.

Prior to salvation, a period of twelve years, I suffered from pressure sores in areas that are paralyzed which required surgery each time. Within the first six months of my salvation I obtained another pressure sore. Pastor Timmy Lucky, at the time, encouraged me with words from Bishop Lee. In the past, Bishop Lee directed a saint that was having an illness to get in every prayer line, no matter what the prayer line was for. By faith and obedience, I did as I was directed; as well as continue with my doctors visits to keep an eye on the wound. Within a few months the prayers were heard and the power of God closed my wound from the inside out. Given my previous medical record of consistent surgeries, the doctors were amazed by my healing.

Prior to salvation I frequently suffered from bladder infections. Once I got saved I began to make this known unto the Lord. Over time I noticed that I was only getting them once a year. Then I noticed that from year 2000 to current I am not having anymore bladder infections. I attribute this to the power of prayer and the stripes Jesus took upon his back.

The Lord saved me by his grace in the Church of the Living God International July of 1993. I was given grace to make all the meetings each year as well as all the General Assemblies. The week before the General Assembly in 1996 I started having stomach pains. I went to the emergency room and they ran some tests and sent me home after a few hours. The following day I was suffering from the same pains, so I went back to the emergency room. They called in a specialist to look at the x-rays. He came and told me that there is a severe blockage in my intestines and he was sending me to surgery immediately. He feared that my intestines would burst and the poisonous toxins would kill me without immediate attention. Outside of fearing for my life, I was very disappointed that I would be missing the General Assembly. I called Pastor Lucky and Elder Lucky to inform them of all that was going on and asked them and the saints to pray for me.

I prayed as best I could during my stay in the hospital. The doctor came in one morning during my first week in the hospital and told me that I healing fast. He was very pleased with my progress to the point that he sent me home. His instructions were for me to go home with minimum activity. I asked him if I could at least go to bible study and church service. He said that was fine. So when the saints came back after the General Assembly, I was there on Tuesday with a great testimony of how the Lord not only saved my life but also raised me up in less time than what was first stated. This is more proof to me of God's power, love, grace and mercy towards me. As well as how God hears the prayers of the righteous and answers them.

That next year's General Assembly, 1997, unbeknownst to me the Lord by grace ordained me as an Elder in the Church of the Living God International.

Make God A Vow

Miracle for Sis Joanne Holt, New Birth, Talboton, GA-Pastor Vicki Johnson

Mother Joanne Holt is a sixty-five year old woman whose ankles would swell continuously. She went back and forth to the doctor, but the medicine that they would prescribe was not helping. Mother Holt noticed the swelling was getting more severe even after taking the medicine. Pastor Victoria Johnson called her out one service to pray for her; she encouraged her to read the word and make God a vow. God honored her prayers and she hasn't had any swelling since then.

THIS SICKNESS IS NOT UNTO DEATH, by Elder Mark Quattlebaum

At the end of October 2003, Elder Mark Quattlebaum was diagnosed with renal kidney failure and was placed in the hospital immediately to be put on dialysis. Due to small rolling veins, Elder Mark had many ports for his dialysis because they would often collapse. For the next few years Elder Mark would find himself in and out of hospitals, and sometimes near death. The Lord was still doing miracles in his body at the time. Being on dialysis, he was not supposed to be using the restroom, but he still was. His blood pressure was still higher than normal but God still kept him until the day he received a call.

Elder Mark was getting tired of going to the hospital for dialysis, and being stuck with needles all the time. He was going to corporate prayer, at noon, as much as he could. One day Bishop White prayed for him and told him, "This sickness is not unto death". Well during 2007, God was moving for him and we did not know it. During this time it looked like hope of getting healed was far away.

There were many occasions that Elder Mark could have gone home to be with the Lord. He had episodes where he had blocked arteries; even his aorta, the main artery to his heart, was blocked. He was in the ICU for a week. Then he had a graft in his left arm and it caused his arm to swell up three times its normal size. God is a miracle worker, and Elder Mark kept remembering what the Bishop said to him, "This sickness is not unto death". The only way I, his wife, held on was through prayer and being with the saints in the Church of the Living God, who prayed with me.

In June 2006, Elder Mark was at Grant hospital down the street from our annual General Assembly. The brothers gathered together to go see him on Monday. He had been in the hospital for about a week and a half. They came and prayed for him and in a couple of days he was able to come to the General Assembly to be with all the saints. God had always kept him through every situation that occurred because he was still remembering and believing the words of Bishop White, "This sickness is not unto death."

One day in May, a patient came into the dialysis clinic to tell everyone he received a kidney. Elder Mark was happy for him, but he it was his desire to get a kidney, so he too could get off dialysis. Well one day, he decided to call the kidney transplant center to see where his name was on the list. Elder Mark discovered that he was not on the list anymore, due to his blood pressure being so high. He was placed back on the list, but there were about one thousand people ahead of him at this time. He was at the bottom of the list, but God said, "This sickness is not unto death," through Bishop White.

In the next few weeks, Elder Mark was getting really tired of going to sit through dialysis for four hours and them sticking him. On this particular day, Elder Mark did not want to go to dialysis; he pressed his way not knowing that God was getting ready to give him a miracle. He still remembered what the Bishop said to him, "This sickness is not unto death". He was preparing for the same routine, as he did on any other day. After being placed on the machine, he received a call from a lady asking if he wanted to receive a kidney. Elder Mark accepted the kidney and was told to get the hospital as soon as possible.

Elder Mark arrived at the hospital, but the kidney had not arrived. The nurse came in to do an examination on him and his blood pressure and creatine was too high. She had to check with the doctor to see if they could proceed with the surgery; the doctor chose to move forward with the surgery. Along with this, the insurance company was not planning to cover the operation. God still was moving for Elder Mark. The doctor was fighting to get this kidney for Elder Mark. The kidney did not come until the next day. The surgery was successful and the kidney started to work within a couple of hours of the surgery. The nurse told us she has not seen anyone use the bathroom as much as he did, immediately after the surgery. God gave him a kidney from heaven because it is still working after five years. We thank God for our family in the Church of the Living God International, who prayed for our family during this time. All the while Elder Mark was still believing,

"THIS SICKNESS THAT WAS NOT UNTO DEATH"

ELDER AND MIN BLANDING

FAMILY LIFE CENTER, CLGI, SUMTER SC

We would like to thank the Lord for giving our son, Daniel, a miracle in his body. Daniel was born six weeks premature. Seconds after being taken to the infant nursery, the nurses noticed he was turning blue. He was immediately rushed to the Newborn Intensive Care Unit, NICU, and remained there for two months. Due to his early arrival, his lungs were underdeveloped. With underdeveloped lungs he was not able to suck, swallow, and breathe at the same time, and had severe reflux. Doctors said if he was in the womb, he would be learning the suck and swallow coordination. While feeding, Daniel would often forget to breathe. The nurses would aid him in breathing again and he had to be fed through tubes. Doctors finally released him from the hospital a day before turning two months old. He was sent home on a breathing (apnea) monitor. This monitor was to be worn at all times to monitor his breathing for seven to ten months. We give God all the glory, honor and praise for miraculously healing his body; he was on the apnea monitor for only two months.

God also gave him a second miracle at the International Missions Convention. He had severe reflux and doctors said that he would eventually grow out of it. After receiving prayer, God immediately healed him. He has not had another reflux episode; as many of you know, he now eats any and everything without any problems. We would like to thank the Lord for what he has done for us and for the prayers of the saints of the CLGI.

Let's Try God

Miracle for Zakiyah Speaks, New & Living Way,

Pastor Kevin Glover

When Zakiyah was little, she had peanut allergies. If she consumed peanuts, her throat would begin to itch, her lips would swell, and she would throw up. This went on until she was about age seven or eight. During the services, I would notice her going to the prayer line, after Elder Nicole Glover preached. When she would go down for prayer she would ask the Lord to heal her of "peanut butter". This went on for weeks at a time. One day, we bought some Nutter Butter cookies from the grocery store. As she was putting away the groceries she said, "Mom, let's try God out and see if I am healed." She opened up the package of cookies and ate one, then another, and another. She did not have any reactions to the peanut butter cookies at all. (submitted 2012)

God is good!!

Man Says No…But God Says Yes

Testimony from Minister Patricia Caslin from New Birth Talbotton, GA, Pastor Vicki Johnson

At the age of 25, I was pregnant with a wonderful daughter. At 26 weeks of pregnancy the doctor determined that I could no longer carry my baby to full term. I had developed a condition called preeclampsia or toxemia. **Preeclampsia** is a disorder that occurs only during pregnancy at the postpartum period, which affects both the mother and the unborn baby. Preeclampsia is a serious condition of pregnancy, and can be particularly dangerous because many of the signs are silent while some symptoms resemble "normal" effects of pregnancy on your body.

I went into the hospital in my sixth month because I had swelling and extremely high blood pressure. The second day in the hospital the doctors determined that I had to have an emergency cesarean birth. The doctor informed my family that my child and I were not going to make it. It was stated that if Bianca made it, she would have several surgeries because her lungs were not fully developed. The saints were at the hospital when the doctor delivered a 1 lb, 8.4 oz baby girl and she did not have to have any surgeries and we are both healthy today.

MIN JAMES BUTLER

WORD OF LIFE, CLGI

August 2007- Doctors diagnosed Sister Ariana Butler with Alopecia Areata, a disease that causes hair loss. She had begun to lose all her hair in the back of her head. One day, in service the Lord used Pastor Jay Johnson, then a minister, to encourage us that she was not going to lose her hair, but that it would grow back. Afterwards, we noticed her hair beginning to grow back. Today she has a head full of hair reaching the middle of her back.

December 2008- Exhorter Lorena Butler was diagnosed with the beginning stages of breast cancer. Mammogram photos were taken of her breast and confirmed that she had cancerous masses in her breast. During the January consecration, she was lifted up in prayer. In February 2009, she went to the doctor to start treatment. A second mammogram was taken, and there were no masses present! She went to her follow up appointment the next week, and it was confirmed she was cancer free.

April 2011- In 2005, doctors informed Exhorter Lorena Butler that she was not going to have any more children. In December 2007 she was positive for being pregnant. Unfortunately, she miscarried the following month. Exhorter Lorena Butler was again positive for being pregnant March 2008, but miscarried in May 2008. On April 18, 2011, Exhorter Lorena Butler gave birth to Sister Annalise Butler.

I pray these testimonies will bless someone, and continue to give God all the glory, honor and praise.

ELDER MARPESSA

Bishop White was visiting Amsterdam while Elder Marpessa was pregnant. When he arrived, he stepped into their house and immediately smelled gas. Bishop White told Brother Marcelo to open all of the doors and windows to let the gas out. They did not smell what Bishop smelled because they had smelled it for so long. Bishop was concerned; he began to wonder how long they had been breathing the gas before he arrived.

With the lingering question, "How long had they been breathing this gas unknowingly", Elder Marpessa went on her twenty-one week doctor's appointment. Bishop White went to the appointment with Minister Marcelo and Elder Marpessa. Elder Marpessa came out and told them that the baby was not responding. Bishop thought, "Oh, it doesn't look good. Lord what is this?" The doctor suggested that she get something to eat to get the baby moving. As they sat eating the baby began to move and Elder Marpessa immediately smiled. "She's moving", Elder Marpessa exclaimed. As of this date, Elder Marpessa and Minister Marcelo have a healthy baby girl.

MINISTER MARCELO

By faith, Brother Marcelo came to the 2012 General Assembly. Brother Marcelo had a chest infection that he was taking antibiotics for. Not only did he have this infection, but he was losing weight due to lack of appetite, constant chills, and very frail. Brother Marcelo pressed his way to one of the Miracle and Healing services.

Bishop White was attending the same Miracle and Healing service. Prior to entering, Bishop White stated that he inquired of the Lord on what to do concerning Brother Marcelo. The Spirit told him, "if he comes to you then you should minister to him, but only if he comes to you". As he walked into service, the Spirit told him "don't go to the pulpit, but sit in the back." Minister Daniel Kennedy asked Bishop what was he going to do concerning Brother Marcelo, and Bishop told Minister Daniel what the Spirit told him to do.

While sitting in the back, Bishop saw Brother Marcelo; he told Minister Daniel to tell Brother Marcelo to come to him. Brother Marcelo came and sat next to Bishop White. The Spirit said, "Lay hands on his stomach and pray". Bishop wanted to pray for him in secret, so if he got healed, he would not get any glory. Bishop told Brother Marcelo he will know when he got healed because he would feel hungry. At the end of one of the Brotherhood Services, Bishop said, "Get him some food now". Brother Marcelo ate and all his food stayed down, and Bishop knew then that the Lord was moving and healing Brother Marcelo.

Prayer of the Righteous

Minister Dorothy Brown, New Birth, Talbotton, GA,

Pastor Vicki Johnson (SEJ)

In 1988, my family and I were in a car wreck; my sister, Minister Leslie Allen, my brother, Deacon James Floyd, and my mother, Missionary Dorothy Floyd. Our car was hit by an eight-teen wheeler truck that flipped over several times. Upon impact, I was thrown from my vehicle. The injuries I sustained were internal bleeding, swelling of the brain, broken legs and a fractured hip. The doctors did not think that me or Deacon James would make it through the night. We survived, but were never to be the same again.

I was hospitalized for seven months, and for about one month I repeatedly slipped in and out of a coma. The doctors informed my mom that she would need to sign papers authorizing the removal of my infected leg. My mom said she prayed all the way to the hospital, and as she walked in, the doctor greeted her saying, "Ms. Floyd, I don't know what happened but the infection is gone." I was told I would need nine months of physical therapy to learn how to walk again, but I only needed five months. After thirty-four surgeries, rods sticking out of my left leg and hip, an infected leg with the risk of amputation, and physical therapy to learn how to walk again, I am a minister in the Church of the Living God International, preaching the word of God with all the activity of my limbs. Miracles and Blessing do happen.

Amen!!

RACHEL BLANDING

FAMILY LIFE CENTER – SE JURISDICTION

Truly we serve a good God and his mercies endure forever! When I was pregnant with Rachel I developed toxemia during the last couple of weeks of pregnancy. Toxemia is pregnancy induced hypertension. Doctors constantly monitored my blood pressure, but it continued to rise. They decided to induce my labor for fear of me having a stroke or losing the baby. I received two different medications; one to induce labor and another to lower my blood pressure. The first medication made my blood pressure spike, the second medication stopped my contractions, and Rachel's heart rate began to drop rapidly. The doctor didn't like my current condition, and decided to put me under anesthesia and perform emergency cesarean. My husband was not permitted to stay in the delivery room under those circumstances. The doctors had a very difficult time getting Rachel to breathe at birth because her body was full of medicine. She then spent the next two days in Newborn Intensive Care Unit detoxifying from the medicine. The doctors told me the next day that we both were very sick and could have died. Truly God is good and we give him all the glory, honor and praise for keeping us. We thank the saints of the Church of the Living God International for lifting us up in prayer.

SIS. MIKE

POWER OF DELIVERANCE - NE JURISDICTION

When Kiara was a baby she had a condition called Labial adhesion, where the opening to her vagina was closed. Her military Pediatrician gave me some cream to apply, to see if the condition could be resolved naturally. If this did not work, I was told she would have to have surgery. The cream was not working, but the General Assembly was approaching! The Saturday of the General Assembly, Bishop Amponsah preached and called a prayer line. I took Kiara down for prayer, and the Lord led me to Dr. White's line. I told him what the doctor said and he asked me if I believed the Lord could do it. Of course I said yes, but I really did not have the faith I should have. Dr. White prayed for Kiara. I told my husband I was going to prove God by not applying the cream and watching to see if the Lord would heal her. Normally, when I missed an application of the cream her labia would close again. After Bishop prayed, her labia opened to the exact size the doctor showed me, if they would have to do the surgery. When we returned home Kiara had her follow up. The Lord gave me the boldness to tell her doctor, "I took her to our annual international convention, asked my Bishop to pray for Kiara, and the Lord healed her." I told the pediatrician that I had not used the cream for, then, over a week. The doctor examined her and said that we would monitor her progress. Kiara has not had a problem since; her doctor wrote in her medical record, 'Bishop prayed for Kiara and the Lord healed her'. Her Pediatrician even came to visit our church!

Christina Bailey's Miracle:

Elder Shirley Bailey and I lost our nephew recently. We were at Grant Hospital when he passed. I was so upset by our loss that I passed out, and was admitted to the hospital for testing. When the nurses tested me, they found I had a bad heart. They also informed me I would need a pace-maker and a defibrillator placed in my heart to stay alive. The testing also determined that I had spots on my lungs and they suspected cancer. I was a smoker for many years prior, and had lost a tremendous amount of weight before being admitted in the hospital; but I refused the test for lung cancer and had the pace-maker and defibrillator inserted into my heart. Elder S. Bailey, my sister, and Minister J. Bailey came to visit me while I was in the hospital. At this time, I was not seeking the Lord and I had no faith that he would heal me, but they still prayed for me during their visit.

I was released from the hospital, and I remember thinking "I am going to die". But as the days past, I started feeling better. At my first doctor's visit, they checked my lungs and told me "We cannot find any spots on your lungs and your heart is getting stronger". I told them, "Of course, you put the pace-maker in." My doctor responded, "No, it takes more time for the heart to gain this much strength." I believe the Lord healed me, and I now have the mind to want to be filled with God's spirit. I attend Pool of Bethesda every Sunday and I attend my sister in law's bible study every Monday.

STEPHENS FAMILY

FAMILY LIFE CENTER, CLGI, SUMTER, SC

Minister Ashley Stephens received a miracle from the Lord during the January 2010 Southeast Jurisdictional Meeting. She had been having severe migraine headaches for about three years, and during the meeting she was having one. She went to the prayer line, Dr. White prayed for her, and she has not had a migraine since. It has now been over one and a half years! PRAISE HIM!

The Stephens family received a miracle from the Lord in 1994. While stationed at Incirlik AB, Turkey and newly saved in CLGI; Minister Kimberly Stephens was pregnant with Michael, and was due any day. We had a doctor appointment on 19 August, 1994 and we were told that Michael was breeched. The doctor said that he was concerned because the cord could choke Michael when he was born. That night we had Friday night service and asked the Bible Study Leaders, Minister Al Edmunds and Minister Bradford Berry, to pray for us concerning Michael being breeched. That night after service, Sister Stephens went to sleep; all night long Michael was turning in her belly. The next day Michael was born a healthy, strapping, baby boy! GOD IS GOOD!

TRACI R. COLEMAN

SWORD OF THE SPIRIT, NE JURISDICTION

Last August, my Dad told us he had been diagnosed with colon cancer. In September, a couple of days before the Missions Convention, he had surgery to remove the tumor; the doctors were pleased with how the surgery went. He started chemotherapy about six weeks later and seemed to be doing okay. At the beginning of this year his health began to decline. He was in and out of the hospital, and the day before our jurisdictional meeting my sister told me he was in the Intensive Care Unit. His heart was beating irregularly, his kidneys were not functioning properly, and the doctors found a bowel blockage. The following Monday my sister told me the doctor asked to meet with the family. Our family met with the doctor that Wednesday. She essentially told us that this was the end for him. They would not do surgery to clear the bowel blockage because his heart would not survive the surgery. She stopped the chemotherapy because the cancer spread while he was receiving treatment, and his illness had become terminal. The doctor recommended that we consider hospice care for him. We met with the hospital social worker and his nurse that Friday. They told us if he made it through the weekend he would go into hospice care the following Monday. After being in hospice for about a week, he had a bowel movement and they immediately began him on a diet of soft foods increasing it over a couple of days to more solid foods. He went into a nursing home from there and in October he went home. He had lost his ability to walk during his stay in the hospital, but he is now able to get around using a cane for support.

"The Miracle Man of Saint Thomas"

Sunday September 22nd, 2013 – It was the last day of the Great 2013 Missions Feast and I came to the meeting looking for something from the Lord, I was going through a little tribulation and I needed a word of comfort and exhortation.

Elder Alston concluded her morning message and it was time for the altar call. I stood at my seat, looking down at the floor, my hands raised as the prayers were going forth. Then a gentle voice spoke to me and said "*You should have Bishop Butler to pray for you"* I immediately recognized the voice of the Spirit. I looked toward the pulpit where Bishop Butler stood with her hands raised, eyes closed and head facing the ceiling. I thought, "She is not even looking in my direction", how will she know I want her to pray for me?" As I struggled inwardly, I never took my eyes off her and just like that, she dropped her hands and came down to the floor. I could hardly believe it! I immediately made my way to her line and was second in her line, with Elder David Kennedy in front of me. As she laid her hands on me immediately she began to prophecy. It was so swift and strong that the tears just began to flow down my cheek, down my neck but her words were so strange. I thought I knew what I needed in my mind but what she gave me what not what I expected:

.......*"Yea I will sustain thy family, yea even the life of thy* ***husband****, I will sustain thy* job *that you will be a light on that campus, yea ye shall draw from a well that shall sustain thee, not* ***many days hence"***... .....

As I walked back to my seat, my white dress stained with tears and makeup. I just kept going over the words in my mind over and over and over again. I was sitting by Pastor Stovall and she just rubbed my back as I sobbed and wept until the end of service. By the end of service, I had regained my composure and was saying goodbye to all of my friends and hugging and kissing saints from various places. The last goodbyes were to our saints from Auburn Opelika Worship Center and Sister Josephine Rule. They were planning to stop through Nashville on their way home and we jokingly went back and forth about their visit. Then, as I was running to the door to get in the truck Sis Josephine Rule pulled me to her, hugged me tight and said "We are stopping in Nashville". I just looked at her and smiled and said “Okay Aunt Phine”. Little did I know that her words were as true and direct as Bishop Butler’s prophecy.

This trip home was a little unusual, we grabbed some fast food, did not stop to eat dinner; did not stop for gas, no bathroom breaks or anything. We arrived home a little after 5pm and we started to clean up to prepare for the visit of the saints coming through Nashville. Elder Eric brought in all the luggage and we were talking about the next thing we needed to do which was going to the grocery store. As I was in Heaven and Faith’s room complaining because Elder Eric did not want to go to the store, I heard a loud *THUD.* I called to Elder Eric – “Babe did you drop something?” I heard no response and came out into the hallway and there he lay on the ground, convulsing. I screamed and dropped to my knees, lifting his head – his eyes had rolled back into his head, white foamy saliva was coming from his mouth and I just began to cry- “Oh my God, No, No, No”. Heaven came running upstairs and I yelled for her to call 911 on my cell phone, the operator came on; she instructed me to turn him on his side, stick my finger in his mouth and press down his tongue. Soon, he stopped convulsing and his breathing was slow and shallow. He was not responsive at **ALL**! The 911 operator instructed me to do chest compressions on his chest until the EMS arrived. As I had the operator on the phone, a text flashed across my screen from Pastor Stovall saying that they were going to keep going and not stop in Nashville. Panic stricken, I used my left hand to bring up another screen while the 911 operator was still on the line and sent a 911 emergency text telling them to come **NOW!**

The EMS arrived shortly thereafter and I dropped to the floor and began to scream and cry, I was scared beyond belief, in shock and in disbelief at what had just taken place. My phone started ringing and through my tears, I told Pastor Stovall that we needed help in Nashville, TN. I had to leave Heaven and Faith at home by themselves in order to follow the ambulance to the hospital.

We arrived at Saint Thomas and after about 45 minutes the nurse came back and told me the most shocking news I had ever heard – “Ms. Russell, your husband had an aneurysm, he has a tremendous amount of blood on his brain, he is really sick, he is going to have to have brain surgery and he is looking at a long hospital stay.” The neurosurgeon came in with the same information – “a lot of blood, a lot of blood, it does not look good, a long road ahead of him, only an 10-15% chance of survival". I was blinded by my tears and could not even believe the words that were coming out of his mouth! As the evening progressed the neurosurgeon decided to wait until morning to do any surgery because they did not expect Elder Eric to live through the night!

By this time, saints had arrived at the hospital and they began to get the word out that Elder Eric needed prayer. The Bishops were all called and I spoke to Bishop White who assured me that he along with the saints would pray. Little did I know that the saints from coast to coast began to pray that night. Many were traveling home from the Missions conference and began to pray on buses, in airports, in their cars, some came to the hospital and went into the chapel to pray. The saints at the Pool of Bethesda gathered at the church and began to call on the name of the Lord. Pastor Jay Johnson sent the word out on the email list –asking the saints to pray. My mind was spinning, I wanted to scream, I wanted to just fall on the floor but the saints would not let me. Pastor Stovall and Sis Josephine Rule literally held me up as I cried and cried and sobbed and wept. My mind was numb, I did not know what to think, how to act, what to say, I did not know anything else to do but lean and depend on the Lord and my church family. The saints were all I had – I had given up mother, father, sister and brothers all for the sake of the gospel. My help truly came from the Lord and from the saints of The Church of the Living God International. (*"When my father and my mother forsake me, then the Lord will take me up", Psalms 27:10)*

Elder Eric had been diagnosed with a stage 4 hemorrhagic aneurysm that bled onto his frontal lobe, causing severe short term memory loss, seizures and loss of cerebral brain functioning. As a result of the bleeding on his brain, he was also experiencing a condition known as hydrocephalus and that is a buildup of cerebral spinal fluid on the brain. His brain was swelling and he was literally dying right before my eyes!

It was the longest night of our lives – sitting in that dark room watching the monitors, watching him in agony and pain. He was experiencing severe seizures on his brain and did not have any cognition about what was happening to him. He had no memory of what happened, he did not know where he was, barely knew who he was and the hardest part of all – he looked right into my eyes and he had no recognition of who I was. I was crushed beyond belief, I did not think that I could feel any worse, but that was the crushing blow that made me sink to a state of despair and helplessness. As I sat through the remainder of the night, I just kept wondering "How is the Lord going to bring us out?" I had taken a look at Elder Eric's chart and there it was in **black ink – "Patient expiration imminent."** But, Thanks be to God who gives us the victory - the prayers of the righteous saints of CLGI kept Elder Eric alive through Sunday evening.

Monday September 23rd, 2013 Elder Eric's surgery was scheduled for 11am. Bishop Smith came by the hospital to pray and as he concluded his prayer Elder Eric had a stroke. The machines started going crazy, he started shaking, and vomiting, the hospital staff rushed into the room and took him into surgery. I could not control myself Pastor Stovall and Sis Josephine took me into the Chapel were Bishop Smith had instructed the saints to gather to pray and Elder Carol Chisolm began to sing. As her voice rang through the chapel and my friends held me close, I just could not help but continue to wonder – "How in the world is the Lord going to make this alright?"

Hours later, the surgery was complete. They had inserted a tube in brain to drain the fluid and blood from his head and a titanium coil was inserted into his head to seal or fix the aneurysm. He was to remain in the Neurological Intensive Care Unit for several, several weeks. His room had to be a low-stimulation environment – no light, no television, no live plant or flowers, no cell phone, no music, no loud or sudden noises. It was a dark and depressive time, visitors only a few at a time, 13 different medications, nurses coming in every hour on the hour, constant 24 hour monitoring. His body was deteriorating rapidly and we needed God to move! At this point the Neurosurgeon only gave him a 35% chance of survival and there was no expectation of a complete 100% recovery, at best they estimated a **yearlong** recovery process.

The saints were coming through Nashville left and right, we needed help and I needed strength. I was weak, scared and so overwhelmed. I had a new job and I did not know if I was going to still have a job – I could not leave the hospital, I stayed night and day! Dr. Crystal Lucky came to Nashville and under the authority of the Holy Ghost she interceded on my behalf with my job. She met with my human resource director and my Associate Dean and through the leading and guiding of the Holy Spirit she was my advocate and by the end of it all they told her to assure me that I did not have to worry about my job!Friday September 27th, 2013 Bishop White came to Saint Thomas Hospital in Nashville, TN. He came through and by the time he left the spirit of life began to move and day by day Elder Eric began to get better. The drainage tube by his bed was turning from dark red, to lighter red, from darker pink to a lighter pink and less and less fluid was filling the cerebral fluid drainage bag. Each CT scan was looking better and better. Bishop TL Lucky was moved by the Holy Spirit to come and sit with Elder Eric for a week in the in the hospital to give me some relief. Then one day, Dr. Scott Standard came into the room on one of his morning rounds and walked in saying "How's my miracle man today?" I looked up and was shocked, I knew Elder Eric was slowly getting better but what exactly did this man mean? Scott Standard is the top neurosurgeon in Nashville, TN and his reputation in Nashville is impeccable and given the severity of Elder Eric's condition – Scott Standard did not expect anything good to come out of this case. The Lord used "Dr. Standard" so that he could lift up a "*Standard*" because the enemy had come in like a flood and tried to overtake us.

Tuesday October 22nd, 2013 God gave Elder Eric Russell the victory and allowed him to walk out of Saint Thomas Hospital on his own 2 feet. Exactly 30 days after the devil tried to take his life and change the course of our family's life forever – God raised up a *Standard* and the saints came together on one accord and when this poor woman cried – the saints prayed and the Lord heard and sent deliverance!

December 23rd, 2013 Ninety days after a stage 4 hemorrhagic aneurism and stroke, Elder Eric has been discharged from all of his therapy – physical, occupational and speech, he has been taken off all medications except for blood pressure medication and he has been medically cleared to resume all normal activities! His last CT scan and angiogram showed – NO EVIDENCE OF HEMORRHAGE!!!!!!

……."*Yea I will sustain thy family, yea even the life of thy* ***husband****, I will sustain thy* job *that you will be a light on that campus, yea ye shall draw from a well that shall sustain thee, not* ***many days hence"***……..

Greetings in the name of our Lord and Savior!!

I just wanted to pass this on to the Saints of CLGI. As you know from the previous email, Minister Mills was diagnosed with an aggressive large B cell lymphoma cancer. She has been through 4 rounds of chemotherapy since early December. Through it all, it has really taken a toll on her body but she is holding on with the Lord's help. She recently completed her 4th round of chemo and the doctors scheduled her for a PET(positron emission tomography) scan this past Thursday. The PET scan illuminates the activity of cancer in the body by a radioactive substance being injected in the bloodstream. The substance is called a tracer to look for disease in the body. When a disease is found it glows on the scan.

On Friday, Sister Mills doctor called us with the results of the PET scan. She informed us how the procedure goes and what they look for on the scan- the illumination specifically. She told us that there was no illumination on the scan. Meaning, there is no activity of cancer in her body. She also stated that the masses have shrunk tremendously and should be completely gone after her next 2 treatments. Saints, we know this is a result of the prayers of the body. Sister Mills was in Stage 4 cancer. In stage 4, the only goal is to prolong life but God has the last word.... We are rejoicing in the Lord and thanking him once again for his miracle working power. God IS A GOOD GOD!!!

Be encouraged, God hears the prayers of CLGI... He is on our side and we are on His side!!

We love you & thank you for all the prayers being sent up on our behalf. God is going to finish this work in her body. Please pass this on to your churches.

Elder Kenneth Mills

www.ingramcontent.com/pod-product-compliance
Ingram Content Group UK Ltd.
Pitfield, Milton Keynes, MK11 3LW, UK
UKHW041919190726
13854UKWH00003B/1335